THE REUTERS FINANCIAL
GLOSSARY

THE REUTERS FINANCIAL GLOSSARY

REUTERS

Published by **Pearson Education**
London · New York · San Francisco · Toronto · Sydney
Tokyo · Singapore · Hong Kong · Cape Town · Madrid
Amsterdam · Munich · Paris · Milan

PEARSON EDUCATION LIMITED

Head Office:
Edinburgh Gate
Harlow
Harlow CM20 2JE
Tel: +44 (0)1279 623623
Fax: +44 (0)1279 431059

London Office:
128 Long Acre
London WC2E 9AN
Tel: +44 (0)20 7447 2000
Fax: +44 (0)20 7240 5771
Website: www.financial-minds.com

....

First published in Great Britain in 2000

© Reuters Limited 2000

ISBN 0 273 65039 4

British Library Cataloguing in Publication Data
A CIP catalogue record for this book can be obtained from the British Library.

10 9 8 7 6 5 4 3

Typeset by Pantek Arts Ltd, Maidstone, Kent
Printed and bound in Great Britain by Redwood Books, Trowbridge, Wilts.

The Publisher's policy is to use paper manufactured from sustainable forests.

FOREWORD

More people than ever before are exposed to business, economics and finance – and to its very own vocabulary. This new edition of the Reuters Financial Glossary aims to make that exposure as painless, useful, even pleasurable, as possible.

Reuters reputation as one of the world's leading news and information companies is built on a global network of financial markets experts. Those experts – our journalists, for the most – make it their business to understand, and then explain, the terminology used in markets and businesses around the globe.

And it is on those journalists that we've called to help define, clearly and concisely, the 3,000 key financial terms that make up this glossary.

Now in its fourth edition, the glossary has been completely overhauled and updated. For the first time we have included illustrations and examples, to add clarity to the text and bring it to life. Another first, we will keep the entries fresh and up to date via our website: www.glossary.reuters.com. The website includes links to the sites of international organizations, exchanges and other relevant sources.

Whether you are trading the markets for a living, or are just an interested bystander, we trust you will find this book a useful companion.

Geert Linnebank
Editor-in-Chief

A

AAA/Aaa Top rating for bonds of the highest quality awarded by the main rating agencies: S&P's, Moody's and Fitch IBCA.

> *See also* Credit Rating, Moody's *and* S&P's

AB Swedish company title: abbreviation of Aktiebolag.

Above the Line ▶ *See* Below the Line.

ABS Asset Backed Securities. Securities collateralized by assets such as car loans and credit card receivables. ABS are created by the process of securitization whereby banks pool types of loans and use them as collateral or security against a bond issue.

> *See also* Securitization

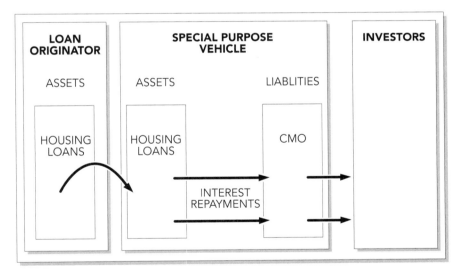

FIGURE 1 ABS

Acceptance House An acceptance house 'accepts' a trade bill at a specified date in the future, meaning it pays the trade bill at a discounted rate.

Account The period during which deals on a stock exchange are done, for settlement on the due account day. The number of days in an account period varies in different countries.

Account Trading The practice of buying and selling securities in a single account period so that settlement is effected by one net payment. This has mostly been the practice in the UK, France, Italy and Belgium.

Accretion Applies to a range of instruments where the notional principal grows in amount over the life of the underlying instrument; the opposite of amortization.
▶ *See also* Amortization.

Accretive A company is described as being accretive if it achieves growth through internal expansion or acquisition.

Accrued Interest The interest accruing on a security since the previous coupon date. If a security is sold between two payment dates, the buyer usually compensates the seller for the interest accrued, either within the price or as a separate payment.
▶ *See also* Simple Interest.

Accumulation/Distribution Analysis A technical analysis indicator that measures the difference between the cumulative amount of buying pressure (accumulation) and the cumulative amount of selling pressure (distribution).
▶ *See also* Technical Analysis.

ACI Association Cambiste Internationale. The professional umbrella organization for a large number of national associations of foreign exchange dealers (cambistes). ▪ **www.aciforex.com** ▪

Acid Test ▶ *See* Quick Ratio.

Acting in Concert Investors working together to achieve the same goal, e.g. to buy all the stock they need to take over a company or purchase the minimum needed so that they can legitimately make an open bid to buy outstanding shares. Sometimes acting in concert is considered illegal. Also known colloquially as a concert party.
▶ *See also* Warehousing.

Active Fund Management A fund is actively managed when securities selection is based on specific ideas and research, and the overall composition of the fund mirrors decisions made at the micro level. It is the opposite of passive management in which a fund aims to match the performance of a market or index, and its constituents mirror the composition of that market or index.

Active X Microsoft programming language, which allows developers to enhance web pages with audio, video and animated graphics.

Activity Indicators Indicators that show which stage of the business cycle the economy may be in. Activity indicators include industrial production, capacity utilization, and volume of retail sales.
▶ *See also* Business Cycle *and* Economic Indicators

Actuals Also called physicals. Refers to the physical commodities available for shipment, storage and manufacture. Actuals that are available for delivery are traded for cash on a spot or forward basis.

Actuary A specialist in statistics and the mathematics of risk, often focused on insurance risks and premiums.

ADB Asian Development Bank. The Bank offers loans, equity investment and technical assistance to its developing nation members. It has 41 members within Asia and 16 outside the region. ▣ **www.adb.org** ▣

ADR American Depositary Receipt. The form in which shares of foreign companies are usually traded on US stock markets.

AE Greek company title: abbreviation of Anonymi Eteria.

Affiliate Two companies are affiliated when one owns less than a majority of the voting stock of the other or if both are subsidiaries of a third company.

After-hours Dealing Dealing taking place after the official close of business on the trading floor of an investment exchange.

AG German company title: abbreviation of Aktiengesellschaft, a joint-stock company.

Against Actuals ▶ *See* Exchange for Physical.

Agent Bank Bank appointed by members of an international lending syndicate to protect a lenders' interests during the life of a loan.
▶ *See also* Syndicate.

Aggregate Demand Total demand for goods and services in the economy. Comprises demand from companies and government for investment goods, demand from local and central government for goods and services and demand from consumers and companies in other countries for exports.

Aggregate Risk Total exposure of a bank to any single customer for both spot and forward contracts.

Aggregate Supply Total supply of goods and services in the economy available to meet aggregate demand. The supply consists of domestically produced goods and imports.

AGM Annual General Meeting. Called some time after the financial year end, inviting shareholders to vote acceptance of the company's annual report, balance sheet and final dividend. Companies often use the meeting to tell shareholders about corporate business prospects in the early months of the new financial year.
▶ *See also* Annual Report *and* Balance Sheet.

AIM Alternative investment market. A UK market for smaller or high-risk companies that do not qualify for a full listing on the London Stock Exchange.
▣ **www.londonstockexchange.com/aim** ▣

Alexander's Filter A technical analysis tool that measures the rate of rise or fall in prices by a percentage price rise or fall over a set period. Buy signals are interpreted by a sufficiently fast rate of increase while sell signals are indicated by a fast rate of decrease.

▷ *See also* Technical Analysis.

All Ordinaries The All Ordinaries Share Price Index or 'All Ords' is the benchmark index for the Australian stock market. It is a capitalization-weighted index consisting of over 300 stocks. ▨ **www.asx.com** ▨

▷ *See also* Capitalization-Weighted Index.

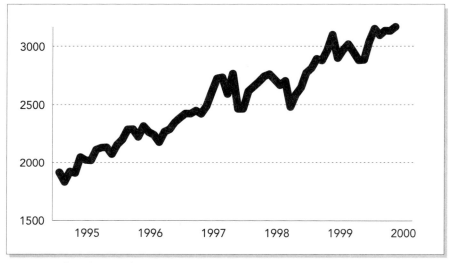

FIGURE 2 All Ordinaries Share Index

Alpha In the context of stock returns, alpha measures the risk-adjusted performance of a security or fund. It is the return on a security in excess of what would be predicted by a risk/return model. In a regression equation, alpha gives the value of the dependent variable when the independent variable has a value of zero, i.e. it gives the intercept of the line with the y-axis.

▷ *See also* CAPM.

Alternative Investment Market ▷ *See* AIM.

American Depositary Receipt ▷ *See* ADR.

American Option An option allowing the holder to exercise at any time the life of the contract, up to and including the expiry date. A variation, called the 'semi-American', is where options can be exercised on only a set number of dates before expiry.

▷ *See also* European Option.

American Petroleum Institute ▷ *See* API.

AMEX American Stock Exchange. ▪ **www.amex.com** ▪

Amortization The reduction of principal or debt at regular intervals. This can be achieved via a purchase or sinking fund. The term is also used to describe the depreciation of fixed assets; the opposite of accretion.
▷ *See also* Depreciation.

AN Norwegian company title: abbreviation of Ansvarlig Firma.

Analyst Generic term used to describe someone who analyses company data, economic data or price charts, in order to make trading recommendations.

Annual General Meeting ▷ *See* AGM.

Annual Rate Compares the average level of a given rate, say inflation, in the current year with the average in the previous year. The benefit of this measure is that it smoothes out unusually large or small changes that may have occurred for a short while during the year.

Annualized Rate Plots the change in an indicator over the whole year if the latest monthly or quarterly figure is presumed to persist for the rest of the year.

Annual Report A status report on the current condition of a company. Issued once a year for shareholders to examine before the AGM .
▷ *See also* AGM.

Annuity An investment that pays a given stream of income for a fixed period of time.

Anti-trust Laws US federal legislation to prevent restraint of free trade and business monopolies.

APEC Asia-Pacific Economic Co-operation. Aims to develop regional trade and co-operation. Members are Australia, Brunei, Canada, Chile, China, Hong Kong, Indonesia, Japan, Malaysia, Mexico, New Zealand, Papua New Guinea, the Philippines, Russia, Singapore, South Korea, Taipei, Taiwan, Thailand, the USA and Vietnam. ▪ **www.apecsec.org.sg** ▪

API American Petroleum Institute. US oil industry institution. Provides key weekly data on US petroleum consumption and stock levels.
▪ **www.api.org** ▪

API Gravity Universally accepted scale, adopted by the API, to express the specific gravity of oils. It serves as a rough measure of quality. The higher the API gravity number, the richer the yield in premium refined products.
▷ *See also* API.

ARA Amsterdam/Rotterdam/Antwerp area. An oil cargo that is offered with cost and freight ARA implies that ports within this area can be considered.

Arbitrage The action of profiting from the correction of price or yield anomalies in markets. Often this will involve taking a position in one market or instrument and an offsetting position in another. As prices or yields move back into line, all positions may be profitably closed out. An arbitrageur is an individual or institution practising arbitrage.

Arithmetic Average Simple average, equal to the sum of all values divided by the total number of values.

Around Par Foreign exchange term used in the forward market when the points are quoted either side of par, i.e. one side of the quotation being at a discount, the other side at a premium.

AS Czech or Slovak company title: abbreviation of Akciova spolecnost.

A/S Danish company title: abbreviation of Aktieselskabet.

ASA Norwegian company title: abbreviation of Aksjeselaskap.

ASEAN Association of South East Asian Nations. It seeks enhanced economic progress and increased stability in the region. Members are Brunei, Indonesia, Malaysia, Myanmar, the Philippines, Singapore, Thailand and Vietnam.

Asia-Pacific Economic Co-operation ▶ *See* APEC.

Asian Option ▶ *See* Average Price Rate Option.

Asian Development Bank ▶ *See* ADB.

Ask A market maker's price to sell a security, currency or any financial instrument. Also known as offer, a two-way price comprises the bid and ask. The difference between the two quotations is the spread.
▶ *See also* Bid.

Assets Assets are tangible items of value such as factories, machinery, financial instruments and intangibles such as goodwill, the title only of a newspaper or a product's brand name.

Asset Allocation The process of distributing investment funds among different kinds of assets, such as stocks, bonds and cash, to achieve the highest expected returns for the lowest possible risk.

Asset-backed Securities ▶ *See* ABS.

Asset Management Also known as liability management, this is the function of controlling assets and liabilities to achieve the optimum return and reduce risk.

Asset Stripping Seeking a profit by buying a company, often when the market price is below the value of the assets, and then selling off all or some of the assets.

Assign To transfer ownership to another party. It usually involves signing a document. In derivatives markets assignment refers to the act of exercising an option.
▶ *See also* Exercise *and* Option.

Associate Formed when two or more companies engage in partnership or joint venture projects.

Association Cambiste Internationale ▶ *See* ACI.

Association of South East Asian Nations ▶ *See* ASEAN.

At Best A buy or sell order indicating it should be carried out at the best possible price available at that moment.

At Par When a security is selling at a price that is equal to face value.

At the Money An option is described as being at the money when the exercise price is approximately the same as the underlying price. 'At the money' options may also be either *in* or *out* of the money. The term is used to describe the exercise price nearest to the underlying.
  ▶ *See also* In the Money, Option *and* Out of the Money.

Auction A public sale of a security whereby the issuer invites authorised dealers to make bids in price or yield until the full amount of the issue is sold.
  ▶ *See also* Dutch Auction.

Audit An official examination of a company's accounts.

Authorized Capital The maximum number of shares that can be issued under a firm's articles of incorporation. This can only be increased only with shareholders' approval.

Average Price/Rate Option An option whose settlement value is based on the difference between the strike and the average of the spot rates over the life of the option. The averaging can be agreed to be taken at any point in the life of the option and readings can be at any specified interval and frequency. Also known as an Asian option.
  ▶ *See also* Option.

BA Norwegian company title: abbreviation of Bergenset Ansvar.

Back Month The futures or options contracts being traded that are furthest from expiry.
> *See also* Futures *and* Option.

Back Office The department in a financial institution that processes deals and handles delivery, settlement and regulatory procedures.
> *See also* Front Office *and* Middle Office.

Back-to-back Loans Arrangement whereby a loan in one currency is set against a loan in another currency. It can be used to avoid or overcome exchange risks and controls. Also known as parallel loans.

Back-up Facility Typically, a bank line of credit used to provide back-up liquidity should an issuer be unable to bankroll the outstanding commercial paper.

Backing and Filling Numerous small rises and falls in a market, usually speculative but showing no major overall change in price levels.

Backpricing Price-setting method in the metal market, whereby a consumer with a long-term contract has the option of fixing the price for a proportion of his contract on the valid LME settlement price.
> *See also* LME.

Backwardation In commodity markets, backwardation is a situation where the cash or near delivery price is at a premium to the price for forward delivery. It is the opposite of contango. Generally in futures markets backwardation is used to describe when a futures price that falls below the cash equivalent. Shortage of supply is often to blame, because demand for the spot or cash product rises sharply, but the futures price stays steady because more supplies are expected in the future.
> *See also* Contango *and* Futures.

Bad Debt When a business recognizes that a debt is unlikely to be repaid, the debt is written off as an expense in the profit and loss account.

Balance of Payments A summary record of a country's net international economic transactions including trade, services, capital movements and unilateral transfers.

Balance of Trade Monetary record of a country's net imports and exports of physical merchandise.

Balance Sheet An accounting statement of a company's assets and liabilities, provided for the benefit of shareholders and regulators. It gives a snapshot, at a specific point of time, of the assets that the company holds and how the assets have been financed.
▶ *See also* Assets/Liabilities.

Balanced Budget The situation in a government's budget where its expenditure matches revenue. Also known as a neutral budget.
▶ *See also* Budget.

Balloon Loan A loan that consists of regular monthly payments with one large (balloon) payment at maturity.

Bandwidth The amount of information or data that can be sent over a network connection within a certain period of time; expressed in bits per second (bps).

Bank Bill A bill of exchange issued or accepted by a bank. It is thus more acceptable than a normal trade bill of exchange because the risk is less and the discount is also smaller.
▶ *See also* Bill of Exchange.

Bank of England ▶ *See* BOE.

Bank for International Settlements ▶ *See* BIS.

Bank Return Weekly or monthly statement issued by a central bank summarising its financial position.

Bankruptcy A court proceeding in which the assets of an insolvent company or individual are liquidated.
▶ *See also* Insolvency *and* Solvency.

Bar Chart A type of chart, widely used by technical analysts and traders, that represents price information on a vertical bar. The top of the bar is the highest price and the bottom of the bar the lowest. A dash on the left-hand side of the bar denotes the opening price and a dash on the right-hand side the closing price.
▶ *See also* Technical Analysis.

Barrels Volume measurement of liquid in the petroleum industry, equal to 42 US gallons or 35 Imperial gallons or about 0.136 tonnes, depending on specific gravity.

Barrels Per Day Recognized worldwide as bpd. It is a measure of the flow of crude oil production from a field or producing company or nation. It can also measure the throughput of crude at a refinery or its capacity or output of refined petroleum products.

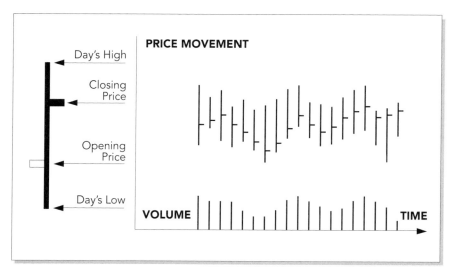

FIGURE 3 Bar chart

Barrier Option An option, which is activated or de-activated once the underlying reaches a set level, known as the barrier. It can be categorized into either trigger or knockout options.
> *See also* Option.

BA Bankers' acceptances, sometimes known as time drafts, are bearer-form short-term non-interest-bearing notes sold at a discount, redeemed by accepting banks for full face value at maturity.
> *See also* Bill of Exchange.

Base Currency The currency that forms the base of a quotation, i.e. the denominator expressed as a unit of one (or sometimes a hundred). For example, the base currency in a US dollar/euro quotation is the dollar, whereas the base currency in the dollar/sterling quote is the pound.

Base Year/Base Date The year chosen to set an index at 100. Any year can be chosen as a base year, but it is generally desirable to use a fairly recent year; widely used in the compilation of macro-economic data.

Base Metals Major industrial non-ferrous metals other than precious metals and minor metals; notably copper, lead, tin, zinc, aluminium, nickel.

Basis The difference between a futures prices and the corresponding underlying cash price. Basis is normally quoted as cash price minus the futures price of the nearest delivery month. There is a high degree of correlation between cash and futures prices but the basis is not constant. A basis trade exploits the expected movements in basis.
> *See also* Backwardation *and* Contango.

FIGURE 4 Basis

Basis Point One hundredth of one per cent (of yield) – 0.01.

Basis Risk The risk that the price of a future will vary from the price of the under-lying cash instrument as expiry approaches.
▷ *See also* Convergence.

Basis Trading ▷ *See* Cash and Carry Trade.

Baud Measures the speed of a modem.

Bear A market player who believes prices will fall and would, therefore, sell a financial instrument with a view to repurchasing it at a lower price. Opposite of a Bull.
▷ *See also* Bull.

Bear Market A market in which prices have been falling for a prolonged period. Opposite of a bull market.
▷ *See also* Bull Market.

Bear Raid An attempt to push down the price of a security, usually by short selling.

Bearer Shares/Bearer Forms Securities which confer ownership with a simple certificate with no central register of owners. Dividends or interest payments are claimed by presenting coupons, clipped from the certificate, to a paying agent. Eurobonds are usually issued in bearer form.

Bearish Holding a belief that prices will fall. A bearish sentiment in the market will, therefore, push prices lower. Opposite of bullish.
▷ *See also* Bullish.

Bed and Breakfast Deal Involves selling a share on a day, shortly before the end of the tax year, and buying it back again the following morning. This can allow shareholders to register a capital loss or profit for tax purposes, but also permits the repurchasing of shares if a rise is expected.

Beige Book ▶ *See* Tan Book.

Bells and Whistles Additional features of a security designed to attract investors and/or reduce issuer costs.

Bellwether An instrument or indicator that is generally seen to be an indicator of the overall market, economy or sector's performance.

Below the Line A term used to describe when an exceptional item is recorded separately in a company's profit and loss account.
  ▶ *See also* Extraordinary Item.

Benchmark A standard used for comparison. A benchmark security is usually the most recently issued security in good size. It sets the standard for the rest of the market. A benchmark issue is highly liquid.

Beta Beta records the risk of a stock related to the risk of the equity market as a whole. A stock's beta measures the volatility of return for a 1 per cent change in the return of the whole market. The higher the stock's beta, the greater its required return. A stock with a beta of more than one tends to be riskier than the market. A stock with a beta of less than one is less risky. High beta stocks tend to be in cyclical sectors such as property and consumer durables. Low beta stocks, also known as defensive stocks, tend to be in non-cyclical sectors such as food retailing and public utilities.

Bhd Malaysian company title: abbreviation of Berhad.

Bid A market maker's price to buy a security or instrument.

Bid-Ask Quote A two-way price comprises a bid and ask/offer. The difference between the two quotes is known as the spread. A spread between the best bid and best offer is called 'the touch'.
  ▶ *See also* Ask and Bid.

Bid Market A market in which there is more interest from buyers than sellers. Opposite of offer market.
  ▶ *See also* Offer Market.

Big Board Colloquial name for the New York Stock Exchange.
  ▶ *See also* NYSE.

Big Figure The stem of a rate. When quoting a price, dealers may only refer to the points (in foreign exchange) or to fractions (in money markets). In the US, the big figure is known as the handle.
  ▶ *See also* Handle.

Bill of Exchange Old financial instrument used to finance international trade. A bill of exchange is an order to pay a specified amount of money to the holder of the bill either at a set future date (a time draft) or on presentation of the bill (a sight draft). Also known as eligible bills, commercial bills, trade bills and BAs.

Binary Option An option that pays out a fixed amount if the underlying reaches the strike level either at expiry or at any time during the life of the option. Also called all-or-nothing option, digital option or one-touch option.
▶ *See also* Option.

Binomial Model An option pricing formula suggested by Cox, Ross, Rubinstein and Sharpe and used primarily to calculate the value of American-style options.
▶ *See also* Option.

BIS Bank for International Settlements. An association of central banks from the G10 countries. The BIS is concerned with safeguarding the stability of international financial markets and ensuring that all banks have sufficient capital to support their operating risks. It acts as a forum for regular meetings of G10 central bank governors. The BIS is colloquially known as the central bank to the world's central banks because it also accepts deposits from them, as well as making advances. ▨ **www.bis.org** ▨
▶ *See also* Central Bank *and* G10.

Black & Scholes Model A widely used option pricing formula for European style options created by Fischer Black and Myron Scholes in 1973.
▶ *See also* Option.

Black Market Economy Transactions not officially recorded due to tax evasion.

Block Trading Large transactions usually performed by institutional buyers or sellers.

Blue-Chip Stock A generic term for the stocks of major companies with sound earnings and dividend records and above-average share performance. Blue chip stocks are also known as income stock.
▶ *See also* Stock.

Blue Sky Laws Laws passed by various US States to Protect the public against securities frauds. New issue offerings have to be registered and full financial details provided. The phrase is thought to derive from a judge's statement that one particular share offer had about as much value as a patch of blue sky.

BOBLs ▶ *See* Bundesobligationen (BOBL).

BOE Bank of England. The UK's central bank. ▨ **www.bankofengland.co.uk** ▨
▶ *See also* Central Bank.

Bollinger Bands Used in technical analysis. Bollinger bands are lines plotted above and below the moving average of the closing prices. These bands narrow and widen in line with volatility – narrow in calm markets and wide in volatile markets. The narrowing of the bands often indicates the start of a new trend, which is confirmed when prices break and close out of the band.

Bollinger bands may be used with any price chart but are most commonly used with bar charts.

▶ *See also* Bar Chart *and* Technical Analysis.

Bolsa Spanish term for stock exchange.

▶ *See also* Stock Exchange.

Bond A legal contract in which an issuer promises to pay holders a specific rate of interest and redeem the contract at face value.

▶ *See also* Bullet Bond *and* Fixed Income.

Bond Equivalent Yield The calculation which converts the yield of a money market instrument such as a Treasury bill into the equivalent yield of a Treasury bond.

▶ *See also* Money Market.

Bond Indenture The complete contract specifying all the terms and conditions of a bond issue.

Bond Washing Selling a security-cum-interest and buying it back after the coupon is paid so as to convert the interest income into a capital gain. This is worthwhile only where lower tax rates apply to capital gains.

▶ *See also* Bond.

Book Trader's record of purchases and sales in one or more financial instruments.

▶ *See also* Matched Book *and* Unmatched Book.

Book Building An exercise by an investment bank lead-managing a new issue to ascertain the likely levels of demand for a security at different prices. It is designed to prevent an issue being undersubscribed because of a large discrepancy between the issue price and the price at which the security starts trading on the secondary market.

Book Entry Securities registered by the issuer, usually in computerized form, and for which there are no physical issues. This method reduces paperwork, expenses and simplifies transfer of ownership.

Bookmark A feature within browsers that allows users to electronically tag certain web pages to make revisiting those pages easier. Sometimes called a favourite.

Book Price The value at which assets were originally entered in the books of a company's balance sheet.

Book Runner The investment firm responsible for looking after the administration of a new bond issue. The book runner is responsible for tasks such as inviting others to subscribe and allocating tranches of the bonds.

Book Value Per Share *See* BVPS.

Borrowing Requirement Net amount of money needed by a government to finance budget deficits and maturing debt.

BOT Buoni Ordinari del Tesoro are Italian Treasury bills with maturities of three, six and twelve months, issued at a discount.

Bottom Fishing Buying of a company's shares by an investor who believes they are not likely to fall much further. Also, when a company buys up loss-making competitors or purchases their assets.

Bottom Line The final, or real, cost or result. The term derives from companies' profit and loss accounts in which the bottom line shows the extent of the profit or loss after all income and expenses have been accounted for.

Bottom Up An investment strategy that relies on stock picking, rather than trying to achieve a balanced weighting in various sectors. If a fund uses a bottom-up approach, it will focus on the performance and management of individual companies rather than general economic or market trends. Opposite of top down.
> *See also* Top Down.

Bought Deal Commitment from an underwriter or lead manager to purchase the whole issue of a security for resale to the secondary market. This method transfers the risk of being unable to sell a whole issue at the offering price from the issuer to the underwriter.

Bourse French term for stock exchange.
> *See also* Stock Exchange.

BPD > *See* Barrels Per Day (bpd).

Brady Bonds These bonds originated as syndicated bank credits to developing countries, denominated in the major Eurocurrencies. During the economic recession of the early 1980s many developing countries ran out of foreign currency to meet their payment obligations on these loans. To restore confidence in the borrowers, much of this debt was converted into negotiable bonds backed by the US Treasury, under a scheme introduced in 1989 by the then US Treasury Secretary Nicholas Brady.

Break-even Point The level at which an existing position will produce neither a loss nor a gain.

Breakout Term used in technical analysis to describe when a price climbs above a resistance level (usually its previous high) or falls below a support level (usually its previous low). Breakouts usually occur when a trend line or formation is broken.
> *See also* Technical Analysis.

Brent Brent blend is a benchmark crude oil against which other crude oils are priced. It is widely used as an indicator of the price of oil beyond energy markets. It is traded on forward markets and is the basis of futures and options contracts listed on the IPE in London. Brent is a blend of crude oils from the Brent and Ninian systems. It is a light, sweet crude that is past its peak in terms of production.
> *See also* Dated Brent, IPE *and* WTI.

Bretton Woods An agreement signed in 1944 at Bretton Woods, New Hampshire, USA, to effect a post-war international monetary system. From this came the creation of the International Monetary Fund and the World Bank. The system was based on fixed exchange rates combined with temporary financing facilities to overcome crises. In 1971 the dollar ceased to be convertible into gold and that element of the Bretton Woods system was superseded by an era of floating currencies.

▶ *See also* IMF *and* World Bank.

Bridging Bridging, or a bridging loan, is made for the short term as an interim aid while awaiting intermediate or long-term financing.

British Thermal Unit *See* BTU.

Broadband A high-frequency, high-capacity method of transmitting data.

Broadening A term used in technical analysis. A price formation with the appearance of a horizontal triangle with widening trend lines so that the triangle base gets wider. Peaks and troughs get successively higher and lower, showing a market that has lost its way.

▶ *See also* Technical Analysis.

Broken Date Any trading date, falling outside the standard periods, traded in the forward markets. Also known as odd date.

▶ *See also* Forwards.

Broker Brokers act as agents for buyers and sellers, for which they charge a commission, or brokerage. There are two main categories of brokers: inter-dealer brokers who only work with specialist market makers, and client or agency brokers who deal on behalf of institutional or retail clients.

Brokerage The commission or fee charged by a broker. In the US, this term is commonly used to refer to a brokerage firm.

Browser Software that allows the user to view websites and applications on the Internet.

B/S Buy after sell limit order. Two orders treated as one, the first order being to sell. If done, the buy order becomes valid.

Bt Hungarian company title: abbreviation of Beteti tarsasag.

BTAN Bons à Taux Annuel Normalisés are French coupon-bearing, fixed-rate Treasury bills with two- and five-year maturities.

B2B Business to Business.

BTF Bons à Taux Fixe et Intérêts Précomptés are French discount Treasury bills with maturities of 13, 26 and 52 weeks. Occasionally, four- and seven-week BTFs are issued outside the calendar and are similar to the US cash-management bills.

BTP Buoni del Tesoro Poliennali are Italian fixed-rate Treasury bonds with maturities of between five and 30 years.

BTU British Thermal Unit. International unit of heating measure.

Buba ▶ *See* Bundesbank.

Bubble A ramping up of asset prices to such a degree that a major reversal or crash is expected.

Budget An itemized forecast of a government's or company's incomes and expenditure for a given future period.

Budget Deficit The amount by which government expenditure exceeds government revenues.
▶ *See also* Budget.

Buffer Stock Stock of commodities held by an international organization to stabilize prices and supplies by buying and selling, using the resources of the stockpile.

BULIS Short-term German money market instruments. Introduced by the Bundesbank in 1993 as an additional instrument of monetary policy to absorb excess liquidity, following the relaxation of minimum reserve requirements for bank lending.
▶ *See also* Reserve Requirements.

Bull A market player who believes prices will rise and would, therefore, purchase a financial instrument with a view to selling it at a higher price. Opposite of a bear.
▶ *See also* Bear.

Bull Market Market in which prices have been rising for a prolonged period. Opposite of bear market.
▶ *See also* Bear Market.

Bull Market Note A floating rate note which is also known as a reverse yield curve note. Traditional floating rate notes have their coupons adjusted higher or lower, following the direction of interest rates. In contrast, Bull market notes pay a higher coupon when rates fall and a lower coupon when rates rise.

Bulldog Bond A bond denominated in sterling, issued in the UK by a foreign borrower.
▶ *See also* Bond.

Bullet Bond Also known as a straight or fixed bond because it has no special features. It pays a fixed rate of interest and is redeemed in full on maturity. Interest is usually paid annually.
▶ *See also* Bond *and* Maturity.

Bulletin Board An electronic message board that allows users to read and post messages.

Bullion Precious metal in non-coin form such as ingots, bars or wafers.

Bullish Holding a belief that prices will rise. A bullish sentiment in the market will therefore push prices higher. Opposite of bearish.
> *See also* Bearish.

Bundesbank The German central bank based in Frankfurt. Its credit policies are set by its central bank council, which normally meets every second Thursday and consists of board members (directorate) and the heads of its regional arms (landeszentralbanken) who run its operations in Germany's 11 federal states.
> *See also* Central Bank.

Bundesobligationen (BOBL) German federal government notes with maturities between two and six years, also known as Kassen. Effectively, replaced by Schätze in 1988.

Bunds Federal government bonds issued with maturities of up to 30 years.
> *See also* Bond.

Bunker Fuel Any fuel oil or diesel fuel used by ships.

Bunny Bond   *See* Multiplier Bond.

Bushel Measure of volume. In the UK, it equals 8 imperial gallons or 36.4 litres for corn, fruit, liquids, etc. In the US it equals 35.3 litres. The weight of a bushel varies according to the commodity involved.

Business Cycle Regular fluctuations in real GDP over time. The cycle has four distinct elements: recession, recovery, peak and slowdown. Business cycles tend to be anywhere from five to 10 years peak to peak.
> *See also* GDP.

Business Risk The risk that a company may not produce the sales and earning growth as forecast.

Busted Convertible A convertible issue of little value because the underlying stock has fallen below the conversion price.

Butane A type of liquefied petroleum gas (LPG).

Butterfly Spread An option strategy involving the simultaneous sale of an *at the money* straddle and purchase of an *out of the money* strangle. Potential gains will be seen if the underlying remains stable while the risk is limited should the underlying move dramatically.
> *See also* At the Money, Option *and* Out of the Money, Straddle, Strangle.

Buy-side Used to describe financial institutions whose primary business is to make investments either for themselves or on behalf of other investors. The opposite of sell-side.
> *See also* Sell-side.

BV Dutch company title: abbreviation of Besloten Vennootschap.

BVBA   Belgian company title: abbreviation of Besloten Vennootschap met Beperkte aansprakelijkheid.

BVPS   Book Value Per Share. A key financial ratio, which is calculated by deducting intangible fixed assets from shareholders' funds. The price of a stock is often related to the book value per share. Companies with high return on equity generally sell for higher multiples of BVPS than companies with lower rates of return.

BVPS (BOOK VALUE PER SHARE)

Book value equals total assets minus total liabilities. It is the same as shareholders' equity. Book value per share (BVPS) equals book value divided by the number of shares outstanding. BVPS is used in the calculation of the price/book ratio, which equals the share price divided by BVPS.

Price/book is the ultimate measure of how much investors think a company's assets are worth. A price/book ratio should be higher than one; otherwise the market is pricing the assets below their replacement value. Companies with price/book ratios well below one automatically become takeover targets, as sector rivals will consider launching a bid for their stock rather than investing in new plant and equipment.

Price/book is especially relevant for capital-intensive manufacturing firms. Service industry companies with few fixed assets typically trade at high price/book ratios.

Formula for BVPS: (Assets – Liabilities)/Number of shares outstanding.
Formula for price/book ratio: share price/BVPS.

Example

According to its 1999 annual report, Reuters has total assets of £2,652 million and total liabilities of £2,051 million. The difference, £601 million, is Reuters book value (also called 'net asset value' or 'shareholders' equity').

Book Value = 2652 – 2051 = 601 million
Book Value Per Share = 601 million/1409 million shares outstanding = 0.4265 GBP.
Price/book ratio: 12.92/0.4265 = 30.29.

C and F Cost and freight, a term is used to indicate when both the costs of the goods and freight charges are included in the price of a commodity.
> *See also* CIF.

CAC-40 The CAC-40 is the principal French stock index covering 40 French equities, although the newer CAC-General, covering 100 stocks, is more widely used. Both of these indices are capitalization-weighted averages. The CAC-40 is the basis for index futures and options traded on the MATIF and MONEP exchanges in Paris. ■ **www.bourse-de-paris.fr** ■
> *See also* Capitalization Weighted Index, MATIF *and* MONEP.

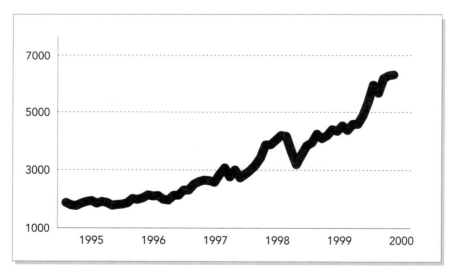

FIGURE 5 CAC-40 share index

Cache A cache is a software function that allows frequently accessed data or pages to be stored on a user's PC to save time connecting to a network.

Calendar Spread ▶ *See* Horizontal Spread.

Call An option which gives the holder the right to buy an underlying instrument.
▶ *See also* Option *and* Put.

Call Money Interest-bearing deposits repayable on demand. This covers both domestic money markets and the Euromarket funds. Also known as day-to-day money or sight money.
▶ *See also* Money Markets.

Callable A callable bond gives the holder the right to early redemption at a given price (redemption price) on a given date (call date).
▶ *See also* Puttable.

Call Provision A clause in a bond's indenture, granting the issuer the right to buy back all or part of an issue prior to the maturity date.

Candlestick Chart A type of price chart widely used by technical analysis. Candlesticks capture the same price information as a bar chart: the open, high, low and close. A thick box (known as the body of the candle) joins the open and close values. Thin lines on either end of the body (known as shadows) join the high and low prices. If the open value is higher than the close value, the body of the candle is solid or coloured. Conversely, if the close is higher than the open then the body of the candle is clear, white or unshaded.
▶ *See also* Bar Chart *and* Technical Analysis.

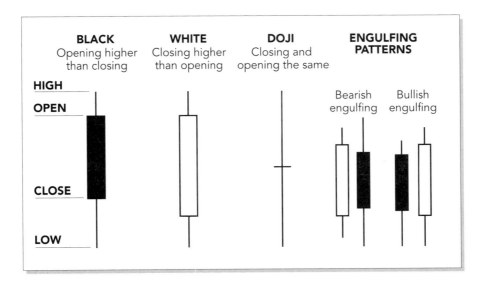

FIGURE 6 Candlestick

CAP The Common Agricultural Policy. This European Union policy was designed to stabilize commodity markets within Europe and ensure regular supplies at reasonable prices while guaranteeing farmers' income. It is implemented through a complex mix of price support mechanisms and export restrictions.
▶ *See also* Union *and* Green Rates.

Cap An interest rate derivative that protects the holder from an increase in interest rates. The holder, by exercising, receives a cash settlement representing the difference between the strike level and the underlying interest rate, should the latter be higher for the set period. Caps normally have a life of between two and five years. The option can be exercised at regular intervals during the life of the cap.
▶ *See also* Derivatives *and* Floor.

Capacity Utilization A macro-economic ratio that compares actual output to potential output. The indicator measures the maximum amount of production that can be utilized during a given period of time, using existing plant and equipment.
▶ *See also* Macro-economics.

Capex ▶ *See* Capital Expenditure.

Capital Economists define capital as assets, other than labour and land, which are required for production. In financial markets capital refers to the financing instruments used principally to acquire capital goods – in particular it refers to debt instruments and equity.
▶ *See also also* Debt *and* Equity.

Capital Account An account in the balance of payments that records movements of capital between domestic and foreign residents. The capital account records changes in the asset and liability position of domestic residents.
▶ *See also* Balance of Payments *and* Current Account.

Capital Adequacy A requirement for banks to have a minimum amount of capital to support their operations. Central banks from the G10 countries agreed in 1988, under the auspices of the BIS, to move towards one standard of capital adequacy.
The BIS rules determine how much and what type of capital commercial banks can raise in the financial markets and what type of loans they are allowed to make.
▶ *See also* BIS, G10 *and* Tier One.

Capital Allowances Allowances on expenditure for capital equipment that can be set against tax .

Capital Asset Pricing Model ▶ *See* CAPM.

Capital Base Issued capital of a company, plus reserves and retained profits.

Capital Controls Government measures that restrict or bar the sending of capital outside a country. The threat of such controls can cause investors and fund managers to withdraw their funds, a reaction is known as capital flight.

Capital Employed Capital used in a business. It may refer to net assets but often includes bank loans and overdrafts.
> *See also* Capital.

Capital Expenditure Payment for the acquisition of a long-term asset. Often known simply as Capex.

Capital Gain Profit from selling or transferring assets at a higher price than their initial cost. Inflation and currency movements can affect the real capital gain.

Capital Goods/Equipment Fixed assets such as plant and machinery used to manufacture goods.
> *See also* Capital.

Capital Intensive A project or production process that uses a relatively large amount of capital.
> *See also* Capital.

Capital Investment Investment in capital equipment such as land, plant or machinery.

Capital Loss Loss when the sale of an asset yields less than the acquisition cost.

Capital Markets > *See* Capital.

Capital Ratios Ratios set by capital adequacy rules. Under the BIS standards commercial banks are required to set aside capital equal to 8 per cent of assets judged to be at risk. Some assets, such as loans to central banks, carry a zero per cent risk weighting. At the other extreme, pure corporate loans are judged as being a 100 per cent risk.
> *See also* BIS *and* Capital Adequacy.

Capital Risk The risk that a company's share price falls in value or becomes worthless, which would result in a loss of capital.
> *See also* Risk.

Capitalization Total market value of a company's issued share capital. The number of shares multiplied by the price.
> *See also* Share *and* Stock.

Capitalization Issue An issue of shares – free to the shareholders – that results from a company transferring money from its reserves to its permanent capital. New shares are distributed to the existing holders in proportion to their holdings. Also known as a bonus or scrip issue.
> *See also* Scrip Issue, Share *and* Stock.

Capitalization-Weighted Index A weighted average of the price relatives of constituent stocks, where each stock is weighted according to its market capitalization relative to the total index.
> *See also* Stock Index.

CAPM Capital Asset Pricing Model. A model tracking the relationship between risk and expected return. Stipulates that the return on a risky asset is equal to the risk-free rate plus a risk premium. The risk premium is the stock's beta multiplied by the difference between the market rate of return and the risk-free rate.

Capped Note A floating rate instrument with an embedded cap that places a maximum coupon rate on the issue.
> *See also* Cap.

Carries LME term for simultaneous matching purchases of one delivery with the sale of another. In other markets, these are termed straddles or switches.
> *See also* LME, Straddle *and* Switch.

Carrying Charge A commodity term that usually refers to warehouse charges, insurance and other incidentals. When used in connection with delivery against futures, will include weighing, sampling, checking of weights, repairing and so forth. Also, used to describe a futures market where price differentials between delivery months fully reflect insurance, storage and interest costs.
> *See also* Futures.

Cartel Group of businesses, organizations or countries who agree, often implicitly, to influence the price or supply of goods. Such a group has less power than a monopoly. In the US, sometimes called a trust.

Cash Collective term for ready money (coins and banknotes) at the bank and in hand, short-term deposits and other liquid assets.

Cash Cow Something that generates a strong and steady flow of income, usually a product or a business.

Cash and Carry Trade An arbitrage position. Typically comprising a long cash position together with a short position in its respective futures contract, whereby the cash price plus the cost of carry is lower than the futures price. Arbitrageurs will, buy cash and 'carry' to the futures date for delivery into the future. Also known as basis trading or buying the basis.
> *See also Arbitrage, Basis and Futures.*

Cash Commodity Physical commodity as distinct to a commodity derivative.
> *See also* Derivatives.

Cash Crop A crop grown for sale rather than for food.

Cash Dividend A dividend paid in cash to a company's shareholders. It is distributed from current earnings or accumulated profits.
> *See also* Dividend.

Cash Equivalent An asset which is so easily and quickly convertible to cash that holding this asset is equivalent to holding cash. A Treasury bill is considered cash equivalent. This term is also used to describe an alternative method of liquidating a position, whereby the seller provides the cash equivalent to the buyer rather than the security itself.

▶ *See also* Cash.

Cash Flow Key data in a company's financial statement. Cash flow is the sum of pre-tax profits and depreciation allowances. The term is also used to describe the stream of funds received by a bond holder from the periodic receipt of interest payments.

Cash Flow Statement The cash flow or flow of funds statement shows how the operations of a company have been financed during the accounting period, and how the financial resources have been used.

▶ *See also* Cash Flow.

Cash Management Bills Treasury bills with maturities ranging from a few days to six months and issued on a discount basis. They are auctioned in the same way as Treasury bills, although not on a regular cycle, and can be announced as late as the auction day itself. Non-competitive bidding is not authorized for these bills.

▶ *See also* Treasury Bill.

Cash Markets Generic term used to describe underlying markets as opposed to derivative ones. The term is also widely used in FX (Foreign Exchange) and debt markets to describe trading in debt instruments with maturities of 12 months or so.

▶ *See also* FX.

Cash Ratios Proportion of cash and related assets to liabilities. In the case of a bank, the ratio of cash to total deposits.

▶ *See also* Cash.

Cash Settlement The most common method of settling financial futures. Cash settlement involves closing out the position as opposed to physically delivering the underlying. Also used to describe a transaction that settles the same day as the trade day.

▶ *See also* Futures.

CBOE The Chicago Board Options Exchange. The world's largest marketplace for listed options, specializing in equity options. ■ **www.cboe.com** ■

▶ *See also* Option.

CBOT The Chicago Board of Trade. The world's oldest futures exchange, specializes in financial and agricultural futures. ■ **www.cbot.com** ■

▶ *See also* Futures.

CCI Certificati di Credito del Tesoro. These are floating rate notes with maturities of seven years, although there have also been maturities of five and ten years. The first coupon is fixed and the following coupons are indexed to six-month or one-year Treasury bill yields.

▶ *See also* Coupon, FRN *and* Maturity.

CD Certificate of Deposit Negotiable money market instruments. A CD is a receipt for funds deposited at a bank or other financial institution for a specified time period and at a specified interest rate. It is quoted on an interest-bearing face-value basis rather than at a discount, and interest is paid at maturity.
▶ *See also* Maturity *and* Money Market.

CEDEL Centrale de Livraison de Valeurs Mobilières, provides clearance/settlements and borrowing/lending of securities and funds through a computerized book-entry system. CEDEL is jointly owned by a co-operative of international banks. ■ **www.cedelinternational.com** ■
▶ *See also* Clearing Bank, Clearing House *and* Clearing System *and* Euroclear.

Centistoke A measure of viscosity in fuel oil.

Central Bank Major regulatory bank in a nation's monetary system. Its role normally includes control of the credit system, note issue, supervision of commercial banks, management of exchange reserves and the national currency's value, as well as acting as the government banker.

Central Bank Intervention The market participation of a central bank to influence monetary conditions when the bank or banks may be seeking to stabilize exchange rates.
▶ *See also* Concerted Intervention *and* Open Market Operations.

CEO Chief executive officer.

Cereals Wheat, oats, barley, rye, rice, maize (corn), millet and sorghum.

Certificate of Deposit ▶ *See* CD.

Certificate of Indebtedness A certificate similar to a Treasury bill with respect to its maturity, but issued with a fixed coupon.
▶ *See also* Coupon *and* Treasury Bill.

CFO Chief financial officer.

CFTC Commodities Futures Trading Commission. The US government agency responsible for regulating domestic futures and options exchanges and their members. ■ **www.cftc.gov** ■
▶ *See also* Futures *and* Option.

Channel Lines Chart lines connecting highs and lows that run parallel to each other. If either line is broken, it may indicate a substantial move in the direction of the breakout.
▶ *See also* Technical Analysis.

Chapter 7 Under US insolvency laws, Chapter 7 deals with involuntary liquidation, where creditors petition to have a debtor judged insolvent by a court. It allows a court appointed interim trustee-wide powers to generally operate the debtor business to prevent loss.
▶ *See also* Insolvency.

Chapter 11 Under US insolvency laws, a debtor who is unable to pay his debts remains in possession of his business and in control of its operations unless a court rules otherwise. The arrangement allows debtors and creditors considerable flexibility in working together to reorganize the business.
▶ *See also* Insolvency.

Charting Used in technical analysis, this set of techniques is used to plot volume, open interest, price movements, settlement prices and other indicators to enable anticipation of future price movements.
▶ *See also* Technical Analysis.

Chart Points Price points or updates on a chart which are connected to form a continuous line.
▶ *See also* Technical Analysis.

Chartist An analyst who uses charts to plot historical trends and to try and project future trends in markets.
▶ *See also* Technical Analysis.

Chatroom Internet term used to describe an electronic conversation forum.

Cheap Rich and Cheap refer to the pricing of a security relative to comparable securities in the secondary market. It is measured using standard deviation. A new issue is considered to be cheap if it is inexpensive compared to the rest of the market.
▶ *See also* Rich Cheap Analysis *and* Standard Deviation.

Cheapest to Deliver ▶ *See* CTD.

Chinese Wall Rules designed to prevent price-sensitive information seeping between dealing, fund management and corporate finance operations within the same investment house. For example, it would not be considered appropriate, and in some countries it is illegal, for a corporate finance team to notify its own in-house market maker of an impending takeover bid.

Choice Price A firm price where the dealer quotes one price for both bid and ask, i.e. quoting with a zero spread. Also called either way.
▶ *See also* Ask, Bid *and* Spread.

Churning Excessive buying and selling on a customer's portfolio allowing a broker who controls an account to earn extra commission.
▶ *See also* Broker.

Cia Spanish company title: abbreviation of Compania and Portuguese company title: abbreviation of Companhia.

Cie French company title: abbreviation of Compagnie.

CIF Cost, insurance and freight. This term is used to indicate when the costs of the goods, as well as insurance and freight charges, are included in the price of a commodity.
▶ *See also* C *and* F.

Circling Pre-selling of an issue by taking orders from prospective customers.

Circuit Breakers Breaks in trading, imposed by exchanges, when prices have fallen by a certain percentage. Circuit breakers are designed to restrict panic selling.

City, the London's financial district.

Clean Price Present value of the cash flow of a bond excluding accrued interest. Basically, the quoted price of a bond.
> *See also* Dirty Price.

Clearing Bank Member bank of a national cheque clearing system. To clear a cheque means to process it through the clearing system so that the payee receives its value. Such systems can also involve clearing financial orders and standardized payment instructions, such as standing orders.

Clearing House A clearing house is the administrative centre of the market through which all transactions are cleared. In addition to administering trades, the clearing house guarantees the performance of contracts. It becomes the counterparty to both the buyer and seller of a contract when a trade has been matched, greatly reducing counterparty risk. Other functions include supervizing the deliveries made against futures contracts and maintaining the margin accounts.
> *See also* Margin.

Clearing System A system that facilitates the transfer of ownership for securities and arranges custody.
> *See also* CEDEL *and* Euroclear.

Closed-end Fund A fund in which there is a fixed amount of authorized share capital, and new shares may not be created on demand. Known as closed-ended publicly quoted funds in the US and investment trusts in the UK.

CME The Chicago Mercantile Exchange. The first futures exchange to trade financial futures. It specializes in short-term interest rate futures and currency futures. ▦ **www.cme.com** ▦
> *See also* Futures.

CMO Collateralized Mortgage Obligations. A mortgage-backed security in which payments by the borrower are passed into a pool from which principal and interest are paid to security holders class by class. CMOs were developed to solve the problem of uncertainty with regard to cash flows. They do this by creating different classes of bonds with different maturities, so that payments from the mortgage holders retire the bonds on a priority basis.
> *See also* Securitization.

Co Widely used abbreviation for company; also Dutch company title.

Co-financing Finance jointly provided for a country both by commercial banks and an international financing institution such as the IMF or the World Bank. In such cases, the commercial banks become more willing lenders.

Cocktail Swap A mixture of different types of swaps. Will often be incorporated to spread the risk on major financing.
> *See also* Swap.

Coffee, Sugar and Cocoa Exchange ▶ *See* CSCE.

Collar Combination of a long cap and a short floor to fix interest payments within a certain range. The premium generated from the sale of the floor may completely or partially finance the premium to be paid for the cap.
> *See also* Cap, Derivatives *and* Floor.

Collateral Assets used as a form of security for bond issuances. In case of default by the borrowers, the lenders (bondholders) have the legal right to claim those assets and sell them off to repay the loan.

Collateralized Mortgage Obligations ▶ *See* CMO.

Combined Option An option comprising at least one call and one put. The components may be exercised or traded separately, although they are originally dealt as one. These strategies may be designed to take advantage of a particular view on the market or to reduce outgoing premium costs. Two common examples of combination options are strangle and straddle strategies.
> *See also* Call, Option Put, Straddle, *and* Strangle.

COMEX Commodity Exchange Inc., a New York exchange trading principally in metal futures.
> *See also* Futures.

Commercial Banks Financial institutions that operate in wholesale and retail banking and allied markets. Commercial banks attract customer deposits and offer cheque-clearing facilities. Hence, the name of clearing banks in the UK or money-centre banks in the US. They are allowed to borrow from their respective central banks when they need short-term funds.
> *See also* Central Bank.

Commercial Paper ▶ *See* CP.

Commission House A term used in futures markets to describe a firm that buys and sells contracts for the accounts of customers. Its income is, therefore, generated by the commission charged for its service.
> *See also* Futures.

Commission Merchant A term used in futures markets to describe a firm or individual that makes a trade, either for another member of an exchange or for a non-member client, but who makes the trade in their own name and becomes liable as principal.
> *See also* Futures.

Commitment Fee A fee paid by a borrower for a lender's commitment to make funds available.

Commitments of Traders A monthly report by the CFTC that shows the total of open positions held by large-volume traders, speculators, hedgers and small position traders.
▶ *See also* CFTC.

Commodity Exchange Inc. ▶ *See* COMEX.

Commodities Futures Trading Commission *See* CFTC.

Common Stock Common stock or ordinary shares represent ownership in a limited liability company. These are companies in which the owners' liabilities are limited to the shareholders' funds and the shareholders usually appoint directors to manage the company on their behalf. Holders of common stock are entitled to dividends when they are declared. They have the last claim on the assets and income of a company.

Competitive Bid Auction Auction method commonly used to issue government bonds, with underwriters submitting bids for certain amounts. The bonds are then allocated according to the level of demand at rates determined by the level of the bids.
▶ *See also* Dutch Auction.

Compounding A process whereby the value of an investment increases exponentially over time due to compound interest.
▶ *See also* Compound Interest.

Compound Interest The interest amount paid or earned on the original principal plus the accumulated interest. Compounding annually means that there is only one period each year in which interest is calculated.
▶ *See also* Simple Interest.

Compound Option An option that grants the holder the right to buy or sell an option at a set price on a predetermined date. If the first option is exercised, the underlying option will then behave as a standard option.
▶ *See also* Option.

Consensus Estimates Averages of estimates of profits per share growth, dividend growth and PER figures supplied by a number of anaysts.

Concerted Intervention Pre-arranged simultaneous intervention in foreign exchange markets, which is carried out by several central banks.
▶ *See also* Central Bank Intervention.

Concert Party ▶ *See* Acting in Concert.

CONSOB Commissione Nazionale per la Società e la Borsa. Italy's official body for regulating and supervising companies and stock exchanges.
▓ **www.consob.it** ▓

Conditionality Conditions imposed when a country draws funds from the IMF related to its credit tranches.
▶ *See also* IMF.

Consolidated Balance Sheet A report showing the financial position of a company and its subsidiaries. Also known as consolidated account.
> *See also* Balance Sheet.

Consolidation Phase A sideways move in the market that generally remains at the same level, despite minor rises and falls; usually has a low steady volume.

Consortium Group of companies formed to promote a common project.

Contango The normal relationahip between a futures market and a spot price where the futures price is higher than the spot price. The opposite of backwardation.
> *See also* Futures *and* Backwardation.

Contingent Option An option for which the holder only pays the premium if the option is exercised. Contingent options are, therefore, a zero-cost option strategy, unless exercised.
> *See also* Option.

Continuation Used in technical analysis, these patterns usually indicate that the sideways price action is more likely to be a pause in an underlying trend (possibly to correct an overbought/oversold condition) and that the next move will be in the direction of the main trend.
> *See also* Technical Analysis.

Contract for Difference An exchange of a fixed and a floating price asset. In FX (Foreign Exchange) markets, the term is used to describe the settlement of the difference between a contract rate and the eventual settlement rate.
> *See also* FX.

Contract Grades Standard grade for each commodity, which must be observed when commodities are delivered against futures contracts. Most contracts have a number of grades or qualities, which result in a premium or discount when delivery actually takes place.
> *See also* Futures.

Contract Month Month in which delivery is due under a futures contract, i.e. when the contract expires.
> *See also* Back Month *and* Futures.

Contrarian Someone who moves or acts in the opposite direction or way to the general trend. For example, a contrarian investor buys stock when the rest of the market is selling.

Convergence The process by which a futures price moves toward the price of the underlying as expiry approaches.
> *See also* Basis Risk *and* Futures.

Conversion The process of converting a convertible security, such as a bond or preferred stock, into common stock.

Conversion Ratio The ratio fixed on the convertibility of a preferred share into a fixed number of common shares, or from a convertible bond into the underlying shares.

Convertible Bond A bond that is convertible into a fixed number of an issuing company's stock at a pre-set conversion price. This price usually represents a premium over the current or average price. Because of this inducement, the bond can carry a lower coupon at par.
> *See also* Bond.

Convexity Like duration, convexity is a measure of the price sensitivity of a bond. It measures the change in modified duration for a change in yield.
> *See also* Duration.

Core Capital ▶ *See* Tier One.

Corp Widely used abbreviation for corporation.

Corporate Dealer A dealer or group of dealers responsible for advising and dealing with corporate customers of their bank who have direct access to the trading room.

Corporate Finance Corporate finance departments advise clients on all aspects of balance sheet risk management, from straightforward currency exposures to more subtle aspects.

Corporate Settlement Market standard for settlement and delivery five business days or seven calendar days from the trade date. Also known as regular way settlement.

Correction A correction in technical analysis refers to a price movement in the opposite direction of the trend. Corrections can occur on both the up and downside of a trend. It is called a correction because the market ultimately reverts to the overall trend.
> *See also* Technical Analysis.

Correlation A statistical term that measures the degree to which two variables move together. A correlation of 1 means that the two variables move together exactly, while a correlation of –1 means that the variables move in exactly the opposite direction from each other.

Cost and Freight ▶ *See* C *and* F.

Cost, Insurance and Freight ▶ *See* CIF.

Cost of Carry The difference between the interest generated on a cash instrument and the cost of funds to finance the position.
> *See also* Positive Carry *and* Negative Carry.

Cost to Close This method calculates the effect of having to liquidate outstanding contracts at prevailing market rates. Used in forward foreign exchange revaluations.

Counter Clockwise Used in technical analysis, this is a chart that plots price against volume over the a given number of periods. Price/volume patterns can be identified and strategies can be planned, based on pattern repetition.

Counter-Cyclical Stock A stock whose market value moves against the rise and fall of the economy. Typically, shares of companies producing necessities whose demand remains relatively constant irrespective of economic cycles; examples would include food retailers.

▶ *See also* Cyclical *and* Cyclical Stock.

Counter Trade The exchange of goods or services where no money is paid. Also known as barter.

Counterparty Risk ▶ *See* Credit Risk.

Country Risk Risks associated with lending funds to, or making an investment in, a particular country. Also known as sovereign risk.

Coupon The interest paid on a bond expressed as a percentage of the face value. If a bond carries a fixed coupon, the interest is paid on an annual or semi-annual basis. The term also describes the detachable certificate entitling the bearer to payment of the interest.

▶ *See also* Bullet Bond *and* Bearer Forms.

Coupon Stripping Detaching the coupons from a bond and trading the principal repayment and coupon amounts separately, thus forming zero coupon bonds.

▶ *See also* Zero Coupon Bonds.

Coupon Swap ▶ *See* Interest Rate Swap.

Covariance A statistical term for the correlation of two variables multiplied by the individual standard deviation for each of the variables. Covariance measures the degree to which two variables move in the same direction.

▶ *See also* Correlation.

Covered Call Writing An option strategy combining a short call position and a long underlying. By owning the underlying on which the option is written, the call is covered (if assigned).

▶ *See also* Option.

Covered Warrant Warrants issued by one institution but on underlying shares that are actually those of another company. For example, Merrill Lynch might issue covered warrants on shares of General Motors. They are covered because the issuer will hold at least some of the underlying stock into which the warrants may be exercised.

Covered warrants are aimed principally at international investors looking for geared exposure to a specific stock, basket of stocks or even an entire index.

▶ *See also* Share, Stock *and* Warrant.

CP Commercial paper. This is a short-term unsecured promissory note issued for a specified amount and maturing on a specified date. CP is a negotiable instrument, typically in bearer form.

CP, like CDs, are a means of raising working capital. In terms of funding costs, the issue of one or another should make no difference since both will produce comparable yields. However, CP tends to be issued with maturities of 30 days or less, to avoid competing with the CD market.

▶ *See also* CD.

CPI Consumer Price Index. The measure of retail inflation.

Crack Spread Calculation showing the theoretical market value of petroleum products that could be obtained from a barrel of crude after the oil is refined or cracked. The crack spread does not represent the refining margin because a barrel of crude yields varying amounts of petroleum products.

Crash A dangerously steep fall in economic conditions or asset prices.

Credit Derivatives Derivative instruments involving credit.

▶ *See also* Derivatives.

Credit Line An agreement by which a bank lends or borrows money up to a specified limit for a set period. The limits on this borrowing are known as credit limits.

Credit Rating Credit ratings measure a borrower's creditworthiness and provide an international framework for comparing the credit quality of issuers and rated debt securities. Rating agencies allocate three kinds of ratings: issuer credit ratings, long-term debt, and short-term debt.

Issuer credit ratings are amongst the most widely watched. They measure the creditworthiness of the borrower including its capacity and willingness to meet financial obligations. A top rating means there is thought to be almost no risk of the borrower failing to pay interest and principal.

The top credit rating issued by the main agencies – Standard & Poor's, Moody's and Fitch IBCA – is AAA or Aaa. This is reserved for a few sovereign and corporate issuers. Ratings are divided into two broad groups – investment grade and speculative (junk) grade. ▦ **www.moodys.com** ▦ ▦ **www.standardpoors.com/ratings/index.htm** ▦ ▦ **www.fitchibca.com** ▦

▶ *See also* AAA, Credit Watch, Downgrade, Moody's *and* S&P.

Credit Risk Risk that an issuer might default on a payment or go into liquidation. Also known as counterparty risk.

Credit Squeeze Occurs when the supply of money is unable to keep up with demand, causing interest rates to rise and exacerbating the borrowing position. Also, a government-imposed situation to rein in excessive spending in macro-economic terms.

Credit Watch A credit rating agency announces that it is putting a company on credit watch, meaning that it expects shortly to issue a lower or higher credit rating.

▶ *See also* Credit Rating.

CRL Portuguese company title: abbreviation of Cooperativa de Reesponsabilidade Limitada.

Cross In the US, a cross is where the broker acts for both the buyer and seller of a security in the same deal. Known in the UK as a put through.

Cross Border Activities in the financial and economic sector that involve movement of goods or negotiations across national borders.

Cross Default Clauses When a lender declares that a loan is in default then, according to the terms of the loan, cross default clauses may be activated automatically. This could mean that other loans and borrowing instruments made to the borrower by the lender – and by other lenders – are also in default.

Cross Listing Shares that are officially listed on more than one stock exchange and, therefore, freely traded away from their domestic centre. They can also appear in cross-border stock market indices.
> *See also* Share *and* Stock.

Cross Rate The exchange rate between two currencies neither of which is the US dollar. However, cross rates are often calculated from the exchange rate of each currency against the dollar.

Crude Oil Oil produced from a reservoir after any associated gas has been removed.
> *See also* Brent *and* WTI.

CSCE The Coffee, Sugar and Cocoa Exchange, a New York futures market, which trades contracts in these three commodities.

CTD Cheapest to Deliver. The security or commodity available in the cash market, which can be delivered most economically against a futures position.
> *See also* Futures.

CTO Certificati del Tesoro con Opzione are Italian fixed-rate notes with six-year maturities, puttable at par after three years. Coupons are paid semi-annually.

Cum Dividend Term used to describe when shares are bought with the right to receive a dividend which has been announced.
> *See also* Ex-Dividend, Stock *and* Share.

Cum All Means a buyer of shares is entitled to all the supplementary advantages attached to a share at the time.

Cumulative Method A method of voting rights which allows the ordinary shareholder to cast votes in any combination for a set number of positions being elected. There is no commitment to equally distribute the votes.
> *See also* Ordinary Share.

Cumulative Preferred Stock A type of preferred share that grants the holder the right to dividend arrears before any payments are made to holders of ordinary shares.
> *See also* Ordinary Share.

Currency Fixings In some markets, a daily meeting is held at which the rates for different currencies are officially fixed by adjusting the buying and selling level to reflect market conditions. The central bank of the relevant country often participates to influence the fix.

Currency Limit The maximum amount a dealer, a group of dealers or a dealing room is allowed to deal per currency.

Currency Risk The potential for losses arising from adverse moves in exchange rates.

Currency Swap An exchange of fixed-interest payments in one currency for those in another, coupled with a commitment to exchange the notional principal amount at the end and possibly at the beginning of the swap agreement at a predetermined exchange rate. The exchange of principal increases the credit risk.

▶ *See also* Swap.

Current Account The current account balance is the sum of the visible trade balance (exports and imports that can be seen) and the invisible balance (credits and debits for services of one kind or another).

▶ *See also* Balance of Payments *and* Capital Account.

Current Assets Corporate assets that can be realized easily. These include stock in trade, work in progress, bank balances and marketable securities. In the US, this can be defined as cash, US government bonds, receivables, monies usually due within one year and inventories.

Current Coupon The prevailing coupon on a floating rate note or other variable rate security.

▶ *See also* Coupon.

Current Earnings Current earnings (or recurrent earnings) are earnings arising from normal company operations, including financial items, but before extraordinary items and taxes. Current earnings are the result of the company's operating earnings (EBIT or earnings before interest and taxes) plus or minus financial items. When analysts forecast earnings per share, they usually forecast current earnings, as they find it hard to predict extraordinary items and taxation.

▶ *See also* Consensus Estimates.

Current Issue ▶ *See* On the Run Issue.

Current Liabilities Short-term working commitments of a company, such as trade creditors, sums due to banks, taxation and dividends payable.

▶ *See also* Assets/Liabilities.

Current Maturity The time remaining to maturity, an important factor in bond valuation.

▶ *See also* Maturity.

Current Ratio Current ratio measures a company's current assets relative to its current liabilities. This gives an indication of its abilities to meet short-term liabilities; the higher the ratio, the more liquid the company.

CURRENT RATIO

Current assets divided by current liabilities. Current assets are made up of cash and cash equivalents ('near cash'), accounts receivable and inventory, while current liabilities are the sum of short-term loans and accounts payable.

The current ratio is a measure of a company's ability to meet its short-term liabilities. Its normal range is between 0.5 and 2.0, but this 'liquidity ratio' must be interpreted with caution. A high ratio could indicate that the company is sitting on too much cash, that it is owed a lot of money by its customers or that it needs to operate with huge amounts of inventory. A low ratio does not necessarily mean the company is a risky creditor. It could mean the company operates in an industry where cash payment is standard (such as restaurants, which typically have little or no accounts receivable), in an industry that operates without much inventory (most service sector companies) or an industry in which customers pay slowly (such as the building sector).

Formula: Current Assets/Current Liabilities

Example

Data from Reuters' 1999 annual report (in million GBP):

Current assets:	1,447
Cash at bank and in hand	119
Short-term investments	490
Accounts receivable	834
Stocks:	4
Current liabilities	1,679

Current ratio: 1,447/1,679 = 0.86.

Current Yield A measure of the return to a bondholder calculated as a ratio of the coupon to the market price. It is simply the annual coupon rate divided by the clean price of the bond.

▷ *See also* YTM.

Curve ▷ *See* Yield Curve.

CUSIP Numbers Committee on Uniform Securities Identification Procedures. Unique identifying numbers assigned to Treasury, federal, municipal and corporate securities.

Custody Traditionally, this term means the storing and safekeeping of securities together with maintaining accurate records of their ownership.
As a result of an increase in cross-border trading, there is a growing need for custody services in several countries. Rather than have several custody services in several countries, investors may prefer to use one global custody service.

Cyberspace The electronic world of created by computer networks.

Cyclical A regular occurrence, something that happens on a periodic basis.

Cyclical stocks Cyclical stocks are those affected by economic cycles such as property and consumer durables. These stocks are generally viewed to be riskier investments and carry a higher beta than non-cyclical stock.
▶ *See also* Beta *and* Counter-Cyclical Stock.

Cylinder ▶ *See* Risk Reversal.

Daily Price Limit The maximum amount, fixed by an exchange, that prices are permitted to rise or fall in one day before trading on a contract is suspended. The daily limit is measured from the previous day's settlement price.
▶ *See also* Limit Up/Limit Down.

Daisy Chain Sequence of deals in which a forward (paper) Brent or Dubai cargo of crude oil is traded ahead of receiving loading dates (known as turning wet). Also known as a paper chain.
▶ *See also* Brent.

Dated Brent Brent crude oil for prompt loading. Dated Brent is a cargo of crude that has been awarded its loading date. This occurs 15 days ahead of loading – or the nearest to 15 days allowing for non-trading days.
▶ *See also* Brent.

Dated Date Date from which interest begins to accrue on a new issue, frequently the issue date.

Dawn Raid Buying a large block of stock in a short time, usually for the buyer to position himself in a possible or actual takeover situation. The purchase often takes place at the start of a trading day.
▶ *See also* Stock *and* Share.

Day Traders Traders who buy and sell assets on their own account but always liquidate their positions at the end of the day. Day traders are known as scalpers in futures markets.

Daycount Conventions Every bond market has its own system of determining the number of days in a year and even the number of days between two coupon dates. These different methods are referred to as daycount conventions and are important when calculating accrued interest and present value (when the next coupon is less than a full coupon period away).
▶ *See also* Coupon.

DAX 100 This is the most widely followed German stock index although it only consists of 30 blue-chip equities and is considered too narrowly based for performance measurement purposes.
Like the S&P 500, the CAC-40 and the FTSE 100, this index is a market capitalization-weighted average index, rather than a simple average.
Unlike these other indices, which only measure change in market prices, the DAX attempts to measure the total return on German equities. In

particular, the DAX includes dividend income and notionally reinvests any dividend income in additional equities in the same proportion as the index. Thus, it is possible for the index to rise even if there is no net change in German equity prices.

Futures and options contracts on the DAX 30 are listed on EUREX.

■ **www.exchange.de** ■

▶ *See also* Capitalization-Weighted Index *and* Eurex.

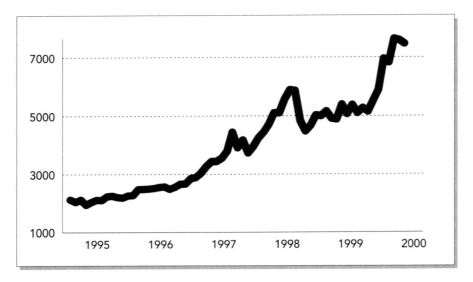

FIGURE 7 DAX share index

DDM Dividend Discount Model. Values common stock as the sum of the present (discounted) values of its estimated future cash flow. It is the share valuation model most readily comparable with bond evaluation, whereby the expected dividend payments on shares are discounted by an appropriate rate.
▶ *See also* Dividend.

DD Slovenian company title: abbreviation of Delniska Druzba.

Dd Croatian company title: abbreviation of Dionicko Drustvo.

Deal Limit The maximum amount that a dealer can trade per transaction.

Dealer An individual or company that trades financial instruments and takes positions for its own account.

Debenture Bond Debt not secured by a specific property but which gives bond-holders the claim of general creditors over all assets that are not specifically pledged elsewhere.

Debt Financial instruments, such as bonds, that represent loans to borrowers (whom investors believe will honour their obligation to repay the interest on and capital of the loan). Debt instruments have a defined life, a maturity date and normally pay a fixed rate of interest.

Debt instruments fall into three broad category of issuer: sovereign, government and corporate.

Debt financing Raising capital by selling debt instruments such as bonds, bills or notes.

Debt for Equity Swap A debtor country buys back its foreign debt at a discount in line with market conditions for local currency that the creditor can then use to invest in one of that nation's companies. The debtor country is then said to have securitized its debt.

Debt/Equity Ratio A ratio that measures a company's debt relative to its equity. Calculated by dividing long-term debt by shareholders' equity.

Debt Service Ratio Cost to a country of servicing its foreign debts and, in particular, debts owed by the public sector and publicly guaranteed debt. The total of interest payments and repayments of principal is expressed as a percentage of export earnings. A level of 20 per cent is normally considered an acceptable maximum but establishing the exact figure is often difficult.

Declaration Date ▶ *See also* Expiry Date.

Default Failure to meet an obligation such as a payment of interest or principal. Technically, the borrower does not default. The initiative comes from the lender who declares the borrower is in default.

Defensive Stock Low beta stocks that are less risky than the overall market. Defensive stocks tend to be in non-cyclical sectors such as food retailing and public utilities.

▶ *See also* Beta.

Deferred Coupon A bond that delays coupon (interest) payment for the first few years, paying it in a lump sum at maturity. It is aimed at investors who want delayed cash flow and who also seek a lower tax bill in early years when their income might be higher than in later years.

▶ *See also* Coupon.

Deficit The difference when expenditure is greater than income. Opposite of surplus.

▶ *See also* Surplus.

Deficit Financing Budgetary policy that produces a deficit and a government borrowing requirement. It can be the direct result of positive government action or failure to control spending.

Deflation A fall in prices

▶ *See also* Disinflation *and* Inflation.

Delivery Price Settlement price set by a clearing house for deliveries of commodities against futures contracts.
> *See also* Clearing House.

Delivery Versus Payment ▶ *See* DVP.

Delta A measure of sensitivity derived from an option pricing model. It measures how much an option's price will change for one unit of change in the underlying price.
> *See also* Option.

Delta Hedging A method used by option writers to hedge the risk exposure of their option book by purchasing or selling the underlying in the spot market in proportion to the delta.

Demerger A company hives off some of its units into a wholly-owned separate concern, which may also be listed on a stock exchange. This can occur following a number of acquisitions of a similar nature that may diverge from a company's mainstream operations.

Depletion Depletion is an accounting measure of the loss of value of a wasting asset such as mines and gas reserves. Reducing the value of tangible assets and intangible assets is known as depreciation and amortization respectively.
> *See also* Amortization *and* Depreciation.

Deposits ▶ *See* Fixed-Term Deposit.

Depository Receipts ▶ *See* ADR.

Depository Trust Corporation ▶ *See* DTC.

Depreciation Depreciation is an accounting measure of the loss of value of an asset as a result of usage, the passage of time, or obsolescense. Depreciation is applied only to tangible assets, amortization is used for intangible assets, and depletion for wasting assets.
> *See also Amortization and Depletion.*

Derivatives Derivatives instruments such as futures, options and swaps are based on underlying cash assets and, in part, derive their value from those assets. In practice, derivatives often drive the underlying market and the volume traded in certain futures and options contacts can outstrip that seen in the underlying cash market.
Derivatives can be traded on an investment exchange or over the counter (OTC).
> *See also* Cap, Collar, Floor, Futures, Option, *and* Swap.

Detachable Warrant Issued as part of a bond but then detached and traded separately in the secondary market. The warrant holder has the right to buy new equity or debt.
> *See also* Warrant.

Devaluation Formal downward adjustment of a currency's official par value or central exchange rate. Opposite of revaluation.
> *See also* Revaluation.

Dilution Reduction in the value of earnings and assets to existing holders of a company's stock caused by an increase in issued stock, which occurs when a rights or free scrip issue is made. In the US, fully diluted earnings per share are earnings after assuming the exercise of warrants and stock options and the conversion of convertible bonds and preferred stock.

Dilutive The effect of reducing a stock's or share's earnings per share.

Dirty Float A system where no official parities for currencies are declared or maintained. In this scenario, a nation's monetary authority intervenes in foreign exchange markets. Also known as a managed float.

Dirty Price Present value of the cash flow of a bond including accrued interest. Also known as gross price.
> *See also* Clean Price.

Discount Generally used to describe when something is selling below its normal price. An asset or fund is described as being at discount when its value is below its market price. In the money markets it is the action of buying financial paper at less than par value. In the foreign exchange markets it is a margin by which the forward rate falls below spot. In the futures market it is referred to as backwardation. Opposite of premium.
> *See also* Backwardation *and* Premium.

Discount Brokerage A brokerage firm that executes orders at a discounted rate of commission rate. Discount brokers tend to offer fewer client services than non-discount or full-service brokers.
> *See also* Broker.

Discount House Term used in the UK to describe an institution acting as an intermediary between the Bank of England and the banking system.

Discount Rate Interest rate at which a central bank will discount government paper or lend money against government paper collateral.
> *See also* Central Bank.

Discount Window The facility set up by central banks who will act as 'lender of last resort' to their commercial banks. Central banks lend at their discretion, and not as a right, to commercial banks at the discount rate.
> *See also* Central Bank.

Discount Yield The yield on a security that sells at a discount.

Discounted Flow Establishes the relative worth of a future investment project by discounting the expected cash flows from the project against its net present value, commonly used in valuing companies and as a component of equity valuation.

Discretionary Account An account for which the broker or bank has a discretionary power of attorney from the holder, either completely or within set limits, to manage on his behalf.

Disinflation A fall in inflation.
▶ *See also* Deflation *and* Inflation.

Disintermediation Process where borrowers or investors bypass banks and other financial intermediaries by directly issuing or buying securities.

Disinvestment Cutting capital investment by disposing of capital goods, such as plant and machinery, or by not replacing capital assets.

Distributed Profits Profits distributed to shareholders via dividend payments.

Diversification Spreading the risk by constructing a portfolio that contains many different investments whose returns are relatively uncorrelated. Thus, risk levels can be reduced without a corresponding reduction in returns.
▶ *See also* Portfolio.

Dividend The part of a company's after-tax earnings, which is distributed to the shareholders. The board of directors of the company recommends how much dividend is paid when at its annual meeting and it is voted through by the shareholders. The dividend is neither automatic nor guaranteed for ordinary shareholders. The dividend can be in the form of cash or shares.

Dividend Cover Extent to which a company's dividend and/or interest disbursement is matched or exceeded by its earnings. Expressed as a multiple. The company's rating in the market increases as the multiple rises.

Dividend Discount Model ▶ *See* DDM.

Dividend Stripping A term used to describe a speculator's strategy whereby shares are purchased shortly before a dividend payment date, based on the belief that a much higher than normal dividend will be paid.
▶ *See also* Dividend.

Dividend Yield Dividend yields are a widely used measure of the income return on a stock. It is the ratio of annualized dividends to the price of a stock; dividends are adjusted to account for any stock splits during the 12-month period. The dividend yield for companies that retain earnings to fund future investments will be low.
▶ *See also* Dividend.

DJIA ▶ Dow Jones Industrial Average. One of the oldest barometers of US equity markets. It is watched by investors worldwide because it is the benchmark for equity prices in the world's largest stock market, and because of the importance of the US economy to the rest of the world.
The index consists of only 30 of the largest US stocks listed on the NYSE. It is calculated as a simple arithmetic average of the constituent stock prices. ▪
www.averages.dowjones.com/home.html ▪
▶ *See also* Arithmetic Average *and* NYSE.

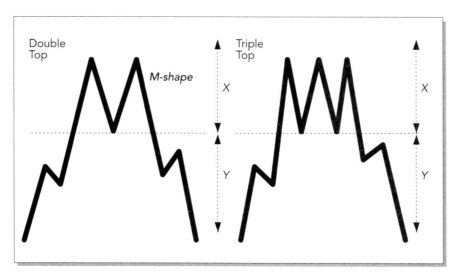

FIGURE 8 Double Top/Triple Top

DNS Domain Name System. System that translates a server's IP address into an alphabetic address such as Reuters.com.

Domain Name Part of the URL that identifes a particular website. All domain names end in a suffix such as .com or .gov, which identifies the top-level domain to which it belongs.
▶ *See also* URL.

Domain Name System ▶ *See* DNS.

Done Dealers' language: verbally confirms a deal.

dot.com Term used to describe a company which is focused on Internet-related business.

Double Top/Bottom A double top is a term, used in technical anlaysis, to describe a reversal pattern that occurs in an uptrending market. A typical top has two prominent peaks at about the same level.
▶ *See also* Technical Analysis.

Dow Jones Industrial Average (DJIA) ▶ *See* DJIA.

Dow Theory Term generally to describe Charles Dow's ideas about stock market behaviour. Dow applied his ideas to the stock market averages (indices) he designed – DJIA and the Dow Jones Transportation Average (DJTA). His theories are widely recognized to be the foundation to many modern technical anlaysis disciplines.
Dow Theory is also used specifically to describe one of Dow's theories – that a major trend in the US stock market has to be confirmed by a parallel change in the DJIA and DJTA.
▶ *See also* Technical Analysis.

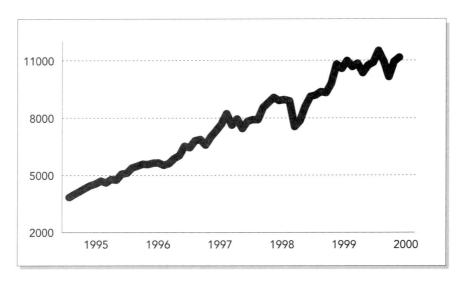

FIGURE 9 Dow Jones Industrial Average share index

Down and In A trigger option that is activated when the price of the underlying falls to a predetermined level. A type of barrier option.
▶ *See also* Option.

Down and Out A knockout option that is cancelled when the price of the underlying falls below a predetermined level. A type of barrier option.
▶ *See also* Option.

Downgrade The reduction of credit rating for a borrowing institution or its debt instruments. Opposite to upgrade.
▶ *See also* Credit Rating *and* Upgrade.

Downsizing The process of reducing the workforce of an organization. Usually involves laying off a significant number of employees.

Downstream Operations such as refining, transportation and marketing, all of which take place after crude is produced.
▶ *See also* Crude Oil.

Downtrend Generally used to describe a falling trend in prices. The term is used more exactly in technical analysis where a trendline has to link four successively lower price points to identify downtrend.
▶ *See also* Technical Analysis *and* Trendline.

Dragon Bonds Bonds issued by Asian companies outside Japan and usually denominated in US dollars. Dragon bonds are usually short-dated, three to five years, and issued by companies who want to expand their range of investors from among Asia's rapidly growing economies.

Drawdown Taking delivery of funds made available from financial institutions. It can include credits from the IMF, Eurocredits from banks or a corporate use of credit granted by a domestic bank.
  ▶ *See also* IMF.

DTB Deutsche Terminborse. Formerly the German futures and options exchange, which merged with Swiss exchange SOFFEX to create EUREX.
  ▶ *See also* EUREX.

DTC Depository Trust Corporation. In the US, shares that are kept in Street Name or Nominee Account may be deposited in a central depository such as the DTC for safekeeping. ▪ **www.nscc.com** ▪

Dual Currency Bond A bond that pays a coupon in one currency, but is redeemed for a fixed amount of another currency, often the dollar. Investors usually get an above-market coupon, but run the risk that, in this example, the dollar would fall below the exchange rate implied when the amount was fixed. These bonds are attractive to borrowers who operate in the redemption currency because they have no long-term exchange rate risk. For other borrowers, the guaranteed exchange rate can be used in a swap, for example, with corporations having liabilities in the currency of issue.

Dual Listing A company which is listed on more than one stock exchange.

Dual Pricing Identical product sold at different prices in different markets or countries.

Dubai Crude A leading benchmark crude oil produced in the United Arab Emirates, used in pricing sour crudes; used predominantly in pricing Middle East crude exports to Asia.

Due Diligence Process The investigation process, performed by investors or lead managers, into the operation and management factors of a potential investment or borrower to verify material facts.

Duration A measure of the average maturity of a bond's cash flows – the coupon payments and principal. Quoted in years, duration indicates the average exposure to market risk. It allows bonds with different coupons and maturities to be compared. Also known as Macauley Duration.
  ▶ *See also* Coupon.

DURATION

Let's say we have a bond which has a 10% coupon, paid annually, that has exactly five years to go before maturity i.e. at 100% of the principal amount. Let us say the present value (PV) or current price of the bond is 116.

To calculate the duration of the bond, we would have the following table, where t equals terms, i.e. years one through five and CF equals

▶

cash flow. The combined present values of each term period will add up to the current bond price, in this case 116.849, and the final column will be each present value times the term.

Coupon = 10%   Redemption price = 100   Calc.date   26/04/00
Annual frequency   PV = 116.849   Mat. date   26/04/05
Term (years) = 5   YTM = 6%

			Duration			**Convexity**		
Period	t	CF	Discount Factor (YTM=6%)	PV	PV*Period	A t*(t+1)*CFt	B (1+y)^(t+2)	A/B
	1	10	0.94340	9.43396	9.43396	20	1.191016	16.792386
	2	10	0.89000	8.89996	17.79993	60	1.26247696	47.52562
	3	10	0.83962	8.39619	25.18858	120	1.33822558	89.670981
	4	10	0.79209	7.92094	31.68375	200	1.41851911	140.99211
	5	110	0.74726	82.19840	410.99200	3300	1.50363026	2164.6885
Sum				**116.849**	**495.098**			**2489.6696**
								21.307

To come up with Macauley Duration, the following calculation is used:
D = SUM (tCF/(1 + y)^t)/PV

If we plug in the numbers from the table we get the following:

D = (10/(1+0.06) + 2*10/(1+0.06)^2 + 3*10/(1+0.06)^3+4*10/(1+0.06)^4 + 5*110/(1+0.06)

That then boils down to the following:
D = 495.098/116.849 = 4.237

So duration in this case, for the single bond is 4.237
D = 4.237

Modified duration equals Macauley Duration divided by the yield to maturity plus one, or Macauley (1+YTM). Given the above numbers that would give us 4.237 divided by (1 plus 0.06), which equals 3.997

Modified duration = Macauley Duration/(1 + YTM)   3.997
MD = 4.237 (1 + 0.06)
MD = 3.997
Convexity = 1/P*SUM t(t+l)*CFt/(1 +y)^(t+2)
Cx = 21.307

Dutch Auction   An auction where the price is lowered gradually – from a price well above the true value – until a responsive bid is seen. This then becomes the price at which the offering is sold. The US Treasury sells its Treasury bills using a similar basis where the bids are termed tenders.
▶ *See also* Treasury Bill.

DVP Delivery Versus Payment. Normal method of settling bond trades whereby delivery of the security is made on the same day as payment is being effected.

Dynamic Time and Sales Alternative term for volume-weighted average price.

> ▶ *See also* VWAP.

E

Early Estimates ▸ *See also* Consensus Estimates.

Early Redemption The repurchase of a bond before maturity by the issuer.

Earnings Per Share ▸ *See* EPS.

Earnings Report An earnings report that differs from the consensus forecast, i.e. what analysts were expecting. Often causes a substantial movement in the stock's price.

EASDAQ A pan-European stock market for trading high-growth companies. EASDAQ was modelled on the US market NASDAQ. ▪ **www.easdaq.be** ▪
▸ *See also* NASDAQ.

EBT Earnings Before Tax.

EBIT Earnings Before Interest and Tax.

EBITDA Earnings Before Interest, Taxes, Depreciation and Amortization.

EBRD European Bank for Reconstruction and Development. A bank set up by the major industralized nations to help centrally planned economies in Central and Eastern Europe move to a free market. ▪ **www.erbd.com** ▪

ECB European Central Bank, which sets monetary policy for the 'Euroland' countries within EMU. Part of the European System of Central Banks. The ECB replaced the European Monetary Institute when the single currency (the Euro) was introduced. ▪ **www.ecb.int** ▪
▸ *See also* EU, EMU *and* Euroland.

ECN Electronic Communications Network. Many ECNs are used for creating electronic stock markets.

ECOFIN Regular gathering of EU economics or finance ministers. The main forum for co-ordination of economic and financial policy within the EU.
▸ *See also* EU.

E-Commerce Electronic commerce, a term used to describe all forms of buying and selling goods electronically.

Econometrics Use of statistical and mathematical methods to verify and develop economic theories. Also covers the development of plans and implementation of policies based on economic findings.

Economic and Monetary Union ▶ *See* EMU.

Economic Indicators Published data that provide information on the current state of an economy. As such they may give clues about the future direction of an economy, sending signals to which consumers, governments, companies and financial markets react. Examples include gross domestic product, consumer price index, money supply, trade balance and unemployment.

Economic Risk The risk associated with changes in exchange rates or local regulations which could favour services or products of a competitor.

Ecu European Currency Unit. A European composite currency based on a basket, with each nation's currency weighted according to each country's share in intra-EU trade, its percentage share of EU GDP and the relative importance of its FX (Foreign Exchange) reserves. The Ecu was replaced by the euro in 1999.

▶ *See also* Euro.

EDSP The Exchange Delivery Settlement Price is the official closing price of a futures contract given by the futures exchange at the end of every trading day. This price is used for marking-to-market purposes and for calculating actual cash settlement amounts required on the expiry date or on the closing out of a futures position.

▶ *See also* Futures *and* Mark to Market.

Effective Exchange Rate Composite exchange rate, normally presented as an index intended to reflect the overall performance of a currency against its main trading partners on a trade-weighted basis.

Efficient Market Hypothesis The theory that all available information about an asset is reflected in the price of that asset.

EFTA The European Free Trade Association, comprising Austria, Finland, Iceland, Norway, Sweden and Switzerland. Liechtenstein is an associate member. The area was established to promote free trade within its members' borders and has a customs union with the EU. ■ **www.efta.int** ■

▶ *See also* EU.

EGM Extraordinary General Meeting.

EIB European Investment Bank. The long-term financing body of the EU. Its main aim is to foster regional development among the member nations and especially to aid less-developed areas on a macro-economic scale. It also provides soft loans to developing countries associated with the EU. ■ **www.eib.org** ■

▶ *See also* EU.

Electronic Communications Network ▶ *See* ECN.

Eligible Bills A bill is said to be eligible when it can be delivered to a central bank at the discount window in return for funds.

▶ *See also* Bill of Exchange.

Elliott Wave Theory A technical analysis theory, which holds that the market follows a repetitive pattern consisting of a five-wave rise followed by a three-wave fall, with these rises and falls completing the cycle. There are many different degrees of trend, but the Elliott Wave theory categorizes nine different trends (or magnitude) ranging from a grand supercycle covering 200 years to a subminuette of only a couple of hours. The eight-wave cycle is constant, regardless of what degree of trend is being considered.
> *See also* Technical Analysis.

E-mail Electronic mail. Messages that are distributed over communications networks.

Embargo Temporary action, generally by one country, to halt shipment of goods into or out of another country.

Emerging Markets Term used to describe the financial markets of developing countries. Definitions vary of which countries are emerging and which are not. However, the emerging market indices compiled by the IFC and Morgan Stanley are often used as benchmarks.
> *See also* IFC *and* MSCI Indices.

EMI European Monetary Institute, precursor to the ECB.
> *See also* ECB.

EMS European Monetary System. A system that links the member states of the EU. The EMS was preceded by a monetary system called the Snake.
> *See also* EU *and* ERM.

EMTN European Medium-Term Notes.
> *See also* MTN.

EMU Economic and Monetary Union in Europe. The process to create a single market within the EU, which allows free movement of people, goods, capital and services. Stage three of EMU saw the introduction of a single currency, the euro in 1999, and the creation of the ECB.
> *See also* ECB, EU *and* Euro.

Encryption A security measure designed to prevent electronically transmitted information from being accessed by anyone other than the intended recipient. Encryption involves coding the information in such a way that only the recipient can decipher it.

Enhanced Scrip Dividend A dividend to shareholders in the form of extra shares which have a market value greater than the value of the dividend. They can usually be sold immediately by the holder.
> *See also* Dividend.

Enlarged Access Method of allowing countries to bend some of the rules in lending by the IMF provided they promise to undertake strong policy measures aimed at redressing payment imbalances.
> *See also* IMF.

Enterprise Value *See* EV.

Enterprise Zone Sites in depressed, mostly inner urban areas, where companies are given favourable taxation treatment and are freed of various planning regulations.

EOE European Options Exchange. A Dutch options exchange that specializes in options on stocks. **www.aex.nl**
  See also Option.

EPS Earnings Per Share. The ratio of attributable profits (net earnings) to ordinary shares.
  The ratio is a key component of the Price Earning Ratio.
  See also P/E ratio.

EPS (EARNINGS PER SHARE)

Net profit divided by the number of ordinary shares outstanding. A company which earned an attributable profit of £10 million in the previous financial year and with two million shares outstanding has an EPS of five pounds.

Historical or trailing EPS are earnings per share for the last available financial year or quarter. Forecast EPS are earnings as forecast by analysts. A consensus forecast is an average or median figure derived from several individual forecasts. EPS is a key component of the Price/Earnings ratio.

Formula: Net Profit/Shares Outstanding.

Example

In 1999 Reuters earned a net profit of 425 million pounds. At the end of the year, it had 1,409 million shares outstanding.
Reuters 1999 EPS = 425/1409 = 0.302 pounds = 30.2 pence.
Forecasts (Consensus EPS estimates provided by Barra):
Reuters 2000 EPS: 27.6 GBp
Reuters 2001 EPS: 30.6 GBp

Equity Used to describe a shareholder's stake in a company. Equity markets are the markets in which shares or stocks are issued and traded.

Equity Financing Selling common or preferred stock to investors to raise funds.

Equity Risk Premium The extra return that the overall stock market or a particular stock must provide over the rate on Treasury bills to compensate for market risk.

Equity options Options that give the holder the right to buy or sell a stock or share.

ERA Exchange Rate Agreement. This is an FX derivative based on a synthetic forward in which settlement is based on two forward rates and not to the spot rate.
> *See also* Derivative, Forwards *and* FXA.

ERM Exchange Rate Mechanism. A system aimed at limiting movements in the currencies of member countries of the European Union before the introduction of the Euro. The grid that was formed in 1979 allowed currencies to fluctuate within bands either side of their fixed central rates.
> *See also* Euro, European Union.

EU European Union. The umbrella term introduced in the Maastricht Treaty to refer to the three-pillar construction in Europe, embracing the European Community and two new areas of co-operation – common foreign and security policy, and justice and home affairs. Has taken over in common usage to refer to the Community in all its aspects. ▦ **www/europa.eu.int** ▦

EUREX The European Derivatives Exchange created in 1998 by the merger of the DTB and Soffex. ▦ **www.eurexchange.com** ▦
> *See also* DTB *and* Soffex.

EURIBOR Euro-Denominated Interbank Offered Rate. The Europe-wide version of the London and Paris interbank offered rates that serves as a benchmark short-term interest rate for European money markets.

Euro-Denominated Interbank Offered Rate ▶ *See* EURIBOR.

Euro The EU's single currency introduced in 1999 by the 11 Euroland countries that joined stage three of EMU. The euro replaced the ecu.
> *See also* Ecu, EMU *and* Euroland.

Eurobond Eurobonds are issued in a specific currency outside the currency's domicile. They are not subject to withholding tax and fall outside the jurisdiction of any one country. The Eurobond market is based in London. Not to be confused with euro-denominated bonds.

Euroclear International clearing organization in Brussels, founded in 1968 that provides clearance/settlement and borrowing/lending of securities and funds through a computerized book-entry system. Euroclear is managed by Morgan Guaranty Trust Company. ▦ **www.euroclear.com** ▦
> *See also* CEDEL.

Eurocredits/Euroloans Large bank credits usually in maturities of three to ten years granted by international bank syndicates put together on an *ad hoc* basis. Lenders are almost exclusively banks and finance companies, thus these credits are not placed with private investors. Interest rates are calculated by adding a margin to interbank-offered rates and usually adjusted every three to six months. Funds for the loans are drawn from the Eurodeposit market.
> *See also* Eurodeposit.

Eurocurrency A currency that is held on deposit outside its country of origin. The most extensively used Eurocurrency is the Eurodollar.

Eurodeposits   Fixed-rate deposits traded wholesale between banks. Eurodeposits have maturities ranging from overnight to one year.
> *See also* Eurocredits.

Eurodollar   ▶ *See* Eurocurrency.

Euroland   Term used to describe the 11 EU countries that joined the third stage of EMU and adopted the euro. The 11 Euroland or Eurozone countries are Austria, Belgium, Finland, France, Germany, Ireland, Italy, Luxembourg, The Netherlands, Portugal and Spain.
> *See also* EU *and* EMU.

Euromarkets   An overall term for international capital markets dealing in Eurobonds, Eurocredits and Eurodeposits.
> *See also Eurobonds, Eurocredits and Eurodeposits.*

European Bank for Reconstruction and Development   ▶ *See EBRD.*

European Central Bank   ▶ *See* ECB.

European Current Unit   ▶ *See* Ecu.

European Derivatives Exchange   ▶ *See* EUREX.

European Free Trade Area   ▶ *See* EFTA.

European Investment Bank   ▶ *See* EIB.

European Monetary Institute   ▶ *See* EMI.

European Monetary System   ▶ *See* EMS.

European Option   An option that the holder can only exercise on the expiry date.
> ▶ *See also* American Option *and* Option.

European Options Exchange   ▶ *See* EOE.

European Union   ▶ *See* EU.

Eurostat   The statistics agency of the EU. The system of actually collating the data is Intrastat. ▨ **www.europa.eu.int/comm/eurostat/** ▨
> ▶ *See also* EU.

Euro STOXX   Shorthand for the Dow Jones Euro STOXX50, one of over 200 indices covering 16 stock markets in Europe compiled by Dow Jones. The Euro STOXX is used as a benchmark for tracking Europe's stock markets. It comprises 50 blue-chip European stocks.
> ▨ **www.dowjones.com/corp/index_directory.htm** ▨

Eurotop 100/300   Two pan-European stock indices compiled by FTSE International. The Eurotop 300 consists of Europe's largest 300 companies and is widely used as a benchmark for tracking the European stock market. The Eurotop 100 covers the 100 most traded large capitalization stocks. ▨ **www.ftse.com** ▨

EV   Enterprise Value. Market capitalization plus net debt. EV/EBITDA has become a very popular ratio to measure the value of listed companies, because the nominator includes a company's debt (and thus a measure of total cost in case of a takeover AND the leverage involved), while the divider (EBITDA) focuses on the company's core earnings power, ignoring elements that may vary depending on local regulations.

▶ *See also* EBITDA.

EVA Economic Value Added. Conceived by consultants Stern Stewart & Co, EVA is a popular method of measuring a company's profitability. EVA is calculated by taking the total cost of capital from post-tax operating profit.

Even Lot Commodity trading unit governed by official exchange price quotations.

Ex Means excluding. Thus ex-cap, ex-div, ex-rights. Indicates that a buyer of shares does not receive a current capitalization issue, a current dividend or a current rights issue. Opposite of cum dividend.

▶ *See also* Cum Dividend.

Ex-All Means a buyer of shares does not receive any of the supplementary benefits attached to a share at the time.

Ex-Dividend Indicates when shares have been bought without the right to receive the dividend, i.e. the seller retains the dividend.

▶ *See also* Cum Dividend.

EX-IM Bank of Japan The Export-import Bank of Japan, a state-owned bank that specializes in loans to developing countries. As a government-backed institution it can borrow on the Japanese markets at favourable rates.

■ **www.japanexim.go.jp** ■

Ex-Rights Term associated with a rights issue, which indicates when stocks are trading without the rights.

▶ *See also* Rights Issue.

Exceptional Item An item within normal business activities, but which is of unusual size. It is usually recorded separately in the profit and loss account.

▶ *See also* Extraordinary Item.

Excess Portfolio Returns Return on a portfolio over and above a 'risk-free' rate such as the yield on US Treasury-bills.

▶ *See also* Portfolio.

Exchange An exchange provides a safe environment in which market participants can trade. Regulated exchanges are like clubs in that they have approved members and a formal set of rules to govern members' behaviour.

Exchange Controls Used to protect and maintain a country's financial position and the value of its currency. The regulations aim to prevent or restrict certain foreign currency transactions, mostly by a country's nationals.

Exchange Delivery Settlement Price ▶ *See* EDSP.

Exchange for Physical Occurs where the buyer of a cash commodity transfers to the seller an equivalent amount of long-futures contracts or receives from him a corresponding amount of short futures at an agreed price. Also termed exchange for cash, and against actuals.

Exchange Rate Agreement ▶ *See* ERA.

Exchange Rate Mechanism *See* ERM.

Exchange-traded contract Standard futures and options listed and traded on a recognized exchange. Opposite to over the counter.
▶ *See also* OTC.

Exercise To make use of the right possessed by the holder of an option. The option holder notifies the writer that they wish to exercise or assign their option. The writer is then obliged to the holder on the terms already agreed – they must buy or sell the underlying asset.
▶ *See also* Assign.

Exercise Price ▶ *See* Strike Price.

Exit bond A long-term bond with a low interest rate, often issued by a less developed country, that gives the buyer the right of exemption from taking part in any subsequent rescheduling. Thus an exit bond allows an investor to convert his existing loans and offers a way out of sovereign lending when the bond is resold or when it matures.

Exotic Term used to describe unusual or complicated financial instruments. The opposition of plain vanilla instruments. In FX (Foreign Exchange) markets the term exotic is used to describe the currencies of emerging market countries.
▶ *See also* Emerging Markets *and* Plain Vanilla.

Expiry Date The date on which delivery takes place on a futures contract. In options trading, it is the date on which a European option can be exercised.
▶ *See also* Futures *and* Options.

Exponential Moving Average A weighted moving average that gives more weight to recent price action.
▶ *See also* Moving Average.

Export Enhancement Programme US programme that allows exporters to receive a subsidy to sell US products to foreign customers at world market prices. The US Department of Agriculture subsidises the difference in the world price and the higher domestic price – which exporters have to pay for the product – in the form of commodities from the Commodity Credit Corporation inventory or cash.

Export Quota Quota set under an international commodity agreement whereby exporting countries of a particular commodity accept limits on their exports. Also a bilateral or multilateral agreement between countries governing exports of industrial or other goods.

Exposure The total amount of credit committed to a borrower or a country. Banks can set rules to prevent overexposure to any single borrower. In trading operations, it is the potential for running a profit or loss from fluctuations in market prices.

Extended Fund Facility Assistance given to IMF member nations with economies suffering from serious balance of payments difficulties due to structural imbalances in production, trade and prices, or economies characterized by slow growth and an inherently weak balance of payments position. Drawings can be made over a period of three years under conditions similar to IMF standby drawings.

 ▶ *See also* IMF.

Extendible Bond A bond on which terms are reset for a further period beyond the initial maturity date. However, both the borrower and the investor will typically have the right to redeem the bonds at these refixings.

Extranet A secure internal network – intranet – that can also be accessed by authorized users outside the organization.

 ▶ *See also* Intranet.

Extraordinary Item A non-recurring item which shows gains or losses outside normal business activities. An extraordinary item is shown in the profit and loss account and affects the balance sheet. It can be, for example, the sale of property or loss from selling part of the company.

 ▶ *See also* Exceptional Item.

Extrapolation The process of determining a rate (or other variable) that lies beyond the range of known rates.

 ▶ *See also* Interpolation.

F

FA Abbreviation of Indonesian company title: Firma

Face Value Apparent worth. The nominal value that appears on the face of the document recording an entitlement, generally a certificate or a bond. For debt instruments, the amount to be repaid at maturity. Known also as par value or nominal value.

Facility Fee Payment made by a borrower to a lender for arranging a loan.

Failure Swing A term used in technical analysis with specific reference to the RSI. A top failure swing occurs if the market is in an uptrend and the RSI is over 70 but the next peak fails to exceed the previous peak. Similarly, a bottom failure swing occurs if the market is in a downtrend and the RSI is below 30 but the next peak fails to fall below the previous peak.
▶ *See also* Technical Analysis.

Fair Average Quality *See* FAQ.

Fair Value A term used in the futures market, which would represent the cash price plus the net cost of carry. The fair-value calculation for an index future is different for every account. It can be defined as any of the following:

- the estimated premium over cash to allow for dividend flows and carrying costs;
- the allowance for expected dividend flows and financing costs involved in holding the contract until expiry;
- how much higher futures should be over a share index after balancing the attractive financing cost of futures against the dividends shareholders receive;
- accounts for financing costs and share dividends;
- the difference between the interest on cash and the dividends paid on the index over the remaining life of the future.

▶ *See also* Futures.

Fallen Angels Bonds which were originally above investment grade but which have subsequently fallen in credit quality.

Fannie Mae Federal National Mortgage Association (FNMA). A stockholder-owned corporation, sponsored by the US Government, that provides funds to the mortgage market primarily by buying mortgages from mortgage originators.

These are held in an investment portfolio or pooled for FNMA members. Purchases are financed by the sale of corporate obligations to private investors. ▪ **www.fanniemae.com** ▪

FAO   Food and Agriculture Organization. An offshoot of the United Nations, which is concerned with the agricultural, forestry and fishing industries.

FAQ   Fair Average Quality. Used in the sale of agricultural commodities, i.e. average grade based on samples rather than on a specific grade.

FASB   Financial Accounting Standards Board. Governs accounting rules in the US. ▪ **www.rutgers.edu/Accounting/raw/fasb/index.html** ▪

FCM   Individual or legal entity registered with the Commodity Futures Trading Commission in the USA who solicits business from others to execute on a listed commodity exchange.

Fed   Shorthand for the US central bank.
    ▶ *See also* Federal Reserve System.

Fed Funds   Reserve balances deposited at the Fed by US commercial banks. These funds can be lent out to other member banks to meet short-term reserve requirements and the rate at which they are lent is known as the Fed Funds rate. The Fed Funds rate is one of two key US interest rates, the other being the discount rate.
    ▶ *See also* Federal Reserve System.

Federal Deposit Insurance Corporation   US federal agency that provides limited guarantees for funds on deposit with member banks. It also takes action to help banks merge or avoid failure. ▪ **www.fdic.gov** ▪

Federal Energy Regulatory Commission   ▶ *See* FERC.

Federal Home Loan Mortgage Corporation   ▶ *See* Freddie Mac.

Federal Open Market Committee   ▶ *See* FOMC.

Federal Reserve Board   Runs the Federal Reserve System. It controls US monetary policy, and oversees the banking industry. Its governors are appointed for 14-year terms while the chairman serves just four years, to allow each president to have their own appointee in the job. The FOMC, a sub-committee of the board, sets US interest rates.
    ▶ *See also* Federal Reserve System *and* FOMC.

Federal Reserve System   This is the central bank system of the US and comprises the Federal Reserve Board, the 12 Federal Reserve Banks and all their member banks. The 12 Fed banks are based in Atlanta, Boston, Chicago, Cleveland, Dallas, Kansas City, Minneapolis, New York, Philadelphia, Richmond, San Francisco and St. Louis. ▪ **www.federalreserve.gov** ▪
    ▶ *See also* Federal Reserve Board *and* FOMC.

Feeds   Classified by the livestock for which they are designed, i.e. poultry, hog, dairy, cattle/sheep, speciality and small animal.

FERC   Federal Energy Regulatory Commission. An agency within the US Department of Energy that oversees regulation of interstate natural gas pipelines and gas prices.   ▓ **www.ferc.fed.us/** ▓

Fibonacci Numbers   A number sequence discovered by a thirteenth century Italian mathematician Leonardo Fibonacci in which the sum of any two consecutive numbers equals the next highest number. The ratio of any number to its next highest number approaches 0.618 after the first four numbers. These numbers are used by technical anlaysts to determine price objectives from percentage retracements.

▶ *See also* Technical Analysis.

FIBOR   The Frankfurt Interbank Offered Rate. This is the rate at which banks are prepared to lend to each other for specified maturities within the Frankfurt market. FIBOR is a key interest rate level used for setting rates for loans and floating rate notes and for calculating cash settlements of certain interest rate derivative instruments.

Fiduciary Money   Money held in trust and invested on behalf of the beneficiary.

File Transfer Protocol ▶ *See* FTP.

Fill or Kill ▶ *See* FOK.

Final Dividend   Dividend paid by a company at the end of its financial year and authorized by shareholders at the AGM.

Financial Centre   A key location in a nation, often its capital, for international and domestic financial transactions, both commercial and between governmental institutions. For example, Tokyo, Paris, Brussels. In London, the financial centre is often referred to as The City or The Square Mile. Among non-capital cities are New York, Chicago, Frankfurt, Milan, Hong Kong, Sydney, Toronto and Osaka.

Financial Accounting Standards Board ▶ *See* FASB.

Financial Intermediation   Financial intermediaries bring together users and suppliers of capital. The term is usually reserved for describing the activities of commercial and investment banks.

Financial Year   The year used for a company's accounting purposes. It can be a calendar year or it can cover a different period. In both cases it can be termed the company's fiscal year.

Fine Ounce   A Troy ounce of gold that is accepted as 995 parts per thousand pure, unless otherwise stated.

Firewall   A combination of hardware and software that creates a security cordon between an organization's internal networks and the Internet.

Firm Order   An order to buy or sell which can be executed without further reference.

First Coupon   The date on which an initial interest payment is due on a bond.

First Notice Day The first date on which notices of intention to deliver actual financial instruments or physical commodities against futures contracts are authorized.

Fiscal Balance The balance of tax revenues and any proceeds of asset sales less government spending. Depending on whether this is a negative or positive value, the balance is described as a fiscal deficit or surplus.

Fiscal Policy Means by which a government influences the economy through its budget by changes in tax and government spending.
> *See also* Monetary Policy.

Fix A term used in foreign exchange and commodity markets to describe the process whereby an official price is set, often on a daily basis.

Fixed Assets Fixed assets are those bought by a company for its continued use for a number of years, rather than for resale. There are three categories of fixed assets – tangible, intangible and investments – which cover things such as land, equipment, a company's logo or brand, and stakes in joint ventures.
> *See also* Assets.

Fixed Capital Similar to fixed assets except purchased out of paid-up capital.

Fixed Exchange Rate A system in which currencies have exchange values with fixed parities, or central-rate relationships with the US dollar or other currencies.

Fixed/Floating Bonds Bonds that pay both fixed- and floating-rate interest at different periods during their life.

Fixed Income The generic term for debt instruments, such as bonds and loans, which pay interest in the form of a coupon. The rate of interest is often fixed, hence the term 'fixed income'.
> *See also* Debt.

Fixed Price Offer New issues are offered on a tender or fixed price reoffer basis. In the latter, the issue is marketed at a predetermined fixed price and coupon. Most new bond issues are offered on this basis.
> *See also* Tender Offer.

Fixed-Term Deposit Deposits placed in the money markets with commercial banks for fixed periods. These deposits are non-negotiable. Maturities extend out to one year and can be as short as overnight.
> *See also* CDs.

Flags/Pennants These price patterns, used in technical analysis, represent brief pauses after a sharp advance or decline that has gone ahead of itself. The market trades in a tight range for a while before running off in the direction of the main trend. Flags and pennants are among the most reliable continuation patterns in technical analysis and rarely produce a trend reversal.
> *See also* Technical Analysis.

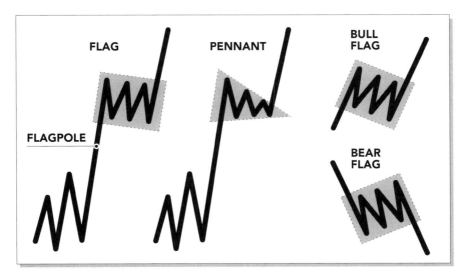

FIGURE 10 Flags and Pennants

Flat A price which is neither rising nor falling; also called sideways. Also, a bond that is trading without accrued interest, such as a bond in default.

Flight to Quality A movement by investors to purchase more secure and higher quality securities, typically Treasuries, which normally occurs if investors are expecting political instability or a deterioration in economic activity.

Floating Debt Debt with a floating interest rate as opposed to fixed.

Floating Exchange Rates A system whereby currencies have no fixed parities and movements are determined by supply and demand.

Floating Rate Bond A bond with a variable interest rate as opposed to fixed.

Floating Rate Note ▶ *See* FRN.

Floor An interest rate derivative which protects the holder from a fall in interest rates. The holder, by exercising, receives a cash settlement representing the difference between the strike level and the underlying interest rate, should the latter be lower. Floors normally have a life of between two and five years. The option can be exercised at regular intervals (every six months, for example) during the life of the floor.
  ▶ *See also* Cap.

Floor Broker The person responsible for accepting orders on an exchange floor and handing them on to a specialist or trader for execution.
  ▶ *See also* Exchange.

Flotation Flotation is the process whereby a company raises new capital. The term is most commonly used to describe when a private company is making its first public issue. This is also known as 'going public' or issuing an IPO.

▶ *See also* IPO.

FNMA ▶ *See* Fannie Mae.

FOB A shipping term, which stands for free on board. If a price quote is FOB this means the costs of the goods and the loading of the ship are included, but not the freight charges of goods at point of embarkation, thus making imports more directly comparable with exports.

FOK Fill or Kill. A limit order to buy or sell that must be cancelled if not carried out immediately.

FOMC The Federal Open Market Committee. This is the 12 member policy committee of the US Federal Reserve Board, which sets official US interest rates and other Federal Reserve guidelines.

▦ **www.federalreserve.gov/FOMC/** ▦

Food and Agriculture Organization ▶ *See* FAO.

Forecast A general term used to describe analysts' predictions for future data including price levels, company earnings and economic indicators.

Force Majeure A force majeure clause is written into contracts to allow contracting parties to be freed from their obligations in the event of an occurrence such as an earthquake, hurricane or a serious labour dispute, which is outside their control.

Foreign Acceptances Similar to domestic bankers acceptances, they are denominated in US dollars and backed by the credit of foreign banks or agencies domiciled in the USA. They usually trade at a yield premium over normal bankers acceptances.

Foreign Bond A bond issued on the domestic capital market by a foreign borrower and denominated in the domestic currency. These bonds have different names according to the currency of issue such as bulldog bond, matador bond, samurai bond and yankee bond.

Foreign Exchange ▶ *See* FX.

Forex Widely used term referring to foreign exchange.

▶ *See also* Foreign Exchange.

Forex Club Umbrella title for the forex organizations which have been formed in various countries as groups of foreign exchange dealers linked by affiliation to the ACI. Each national organization is fully autonomous within the framework of the ACI charter and bylaws.

▶ *See also* ACI.

Forwards A forward is an agreement to buy or sell a financial asset at a future date for a fixed price. Unlike futures, forwards are not standardized contracts and are traded OTC rather than on an exchange.

▶ *See also* Futures *and* OTC.

Forward Margin Discount or premium between the spot and forward rates for a forward foreign exchange transaction that represents the interest-rate differential between the two currencies traded.

> *See also* Discount *and* Premium.

Forward Market Markets that deliver and settle on a date other than spot. The term is often used to describe the forward FX (Foreign Exchange) market, which is one of the most liquid forward markets.

> *See also* Forwards.

Franc Zone A zone that embraces a number of emerging markets all of which have linked their currencies to the French franc and hold most of their currency reserves in francs. Members include Burkina Faso, Cameroon, the Ivory Coast, Niger, New Caledonia and French Polynesia.

FRA Forward Rate Agreement. An interest-rate derivative allowing investors and borrowers to set the interest rate on a short-term investment or loan in advance for a predetermined period.

> *See also* Derivatives.

Freddie Mac Federal Home Loan Mortgage Corporation. Various US savings institutions own the stock of this corporation, which purchases residential mortgages from lenders, forms bundles of securities backed by the pools of mortgages and then offers the securities to the public.

> **www.freddiemac.com**

Free Delivery Method of settlement in which the securities are delivered before payment is effected.

Free to Trade ▸ *See* W/I.

Free Trade Zone A designated extra-territorial area within a country in which businesses can operate free of government hindrance, customs duties or currency restrictions. There is usually a tax-free profits element for a set period. Also known as a free trade processing zone and a foreign trade zone.

Frictional Unemployment Unemployment caused by the time it takes workers to search for a job, sometimes inevitable in a changing economy.

> *See also* Unemployment.

FRN Floating rate note. A medium-term debt instrument that pays regular coupons but those coupons are not fixed. Instead the coupon rates are adjusted periodically in line with short-term interest rates such as LIBOR.

> *See also* Coupon *and* LIBOR.

Front-end Fees On a loan, lead and co-lead managers receive front-end fees from a borrower for making arrangements and fees for servicing the loan i.e. arranging interest payments and principal repayments.

> *See also* Lead Manager/Underwriter.

Front Office Term used to describe the front-line-dealing staff and support functions of a financial institution.

> *See also* Back Office *and* Middle Office.

Frozen Assets Assets, balances or credits temporarily blocked or immobilised due to political circumstances such as war or legal action.

FTP File Transfer Protocol. A common method used to transmit electronic files from one computer to another.

FTSE 100 The FTSE 100 is the benchmark index for equity prices on the London Stock Exchange. Known as the 'Footsie' it includes 100 of the largest UK stocks, by market capitalization, accounting for about 70 per cent of stock turnover. The FTSE is a capitalization-weighted index and is the basis for index futures and options contracts traded on LIFFE. ▪ **www.ftse.com** ▪
  ▶ *See also* LIFFE *and* LSE.

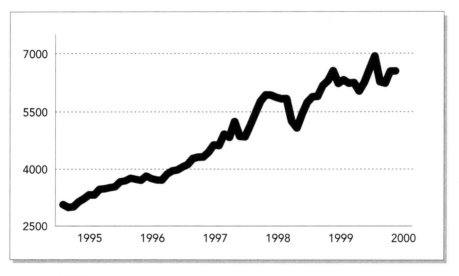

FIGURE 11 FTSE

Fuel Oil Heavy distillates from the oil refining process. Used as fuel for power stations, industry and marine boilers.

Fully Diluted EPS An EPS figure calculated by dividing earnings by a larger amount of outstanding shares, having assumed full share issues to forthcoming of all convertibles, options, warrants and convertible preferred shares. This leads to a greater dilution of the EPS figure.

Fund A pool of money which is invested with a fund manager who then manages that money using a range of investment criteria.

Fund Manager An institution, or individual, involved in investing funds, either on their own account or on behalf of others.

Fundamental Analysis A method of forecasting prices based on research of company performance and basic economic, political and environmental factors. Unlike technical analysis, fundamental analysis focuses on what should happen to prices, not what has happened to them. Fundamental analysts base their forecasts on factors such supply and demand, economic statistics, government policies and the financial accounts of companies.

▶ *See also* Quantitative Analysis *and* Technical Analysis.

Fungible The term used to describe when one instrument is identical to, and therefore interchangeable with another. A fungible bond is a new issue which is attached to an existing issue in the sense that it has the same specifications, other than price. If a bond is fungible, it can be exchanged for an existing bond with the same characteristics.

▶ *See also* Bond.

Future value The expected value, at a set date in the future, of a payment or series of payments that are invested at a specific rate of interest until that date.

Futures A future is an undertaking to buy or sell a standard quantity of a financial asset or commodity at a future date and a fixed price. Futures resemble forwards but there are two fundamental characteristics that distinguish them from forwards – futures are standardized contracts and they have to be traded on a recognized exchange.

Every contract has standardized terms that dictate the size, the unit of price quotation, delivery date and contract months. Price movements are often expressed in ticks – a tick being the smallest unit of quotation. Delivery of a future is rare. As the delivery date draws near, most investors close out their positions by undertaking an equal and opposite trade.

Futures markets bring together hedgers who wish to protect themselves against the rise or fall of prices, and speculators who are trying to benefit from such movements. A clearing house acts at the counterparty in every transaction to protect against the risk of default.

Futures developed as a method for establishing forward purchase prices and managing price instability caused by seasonal factors in agricultural markets. Today, interest rate and stock index futures attract the greatest volume.

▶ *See also* Clearing House, Forwards, Hedging, Margin, Option, OTC *and* Tick.

Futures Commission Merchant ▶ *See* FCM.

Futures Pit Area on the floor of a futures exchange where trading takes place by way of open outcry.

▶ *See also* Open Outcry.

FX The Foreign Exchange FX markets that deal in the exchange of deposits in different currencies for varying effective 'value' dates. Most transactions are for 12 months or less, and are in the form of spot (cash), forwards, futures and options.

FX rates refer to the number of units of one currency needed to buy another.

▶ *See also* Spot Market, Forwards, Futures *and* Option.

FX Swap A foreign exchange swap is a simultaneous purchase and sale, or vice versa, of identical amounts of one currency for another with two different value dates (normally spot to forward). The price of a swap is quoted in forward points.

▶ *See also* Swap.

FXA A Forward Exchange Agreement. A currency derivative in which settlement is based on the difference between the forward rate on the start date of the contract and the spot rate at settlement.

▶ *See also* Derivatives *and* ERA.

G3 The world's leading industrial nations – Germany, Japan and the USA.

G7 A forum for the world's leading industrial nations to meet and discuss policy. The G7 members are Canada, France, Germany, Italy, Japan, the UK and the USA. The same group has been nicknamed the G8 on occasions when Russia has attended meetings.

G10 The G7 countries plus four others: Belgium, The Netherlands, Sweden and Switzerland. Despite having 11 members, the group is still known as G10. It aims to co-ordinate monetary and fiscal policies to form a more stable world economic system.
▶ *See also* G7.

G24 An informal grouping of 24 developing nations.

G30 A group of industry leaders, bankers, central bankers and academics that discusses and studies economic and financial market issues.

GAAP Generally accepted accounting principles. Procedures and rules that define accounting practice.

GAB General Arrangements to Borrow. An agreement between the G10 nations and Switzerland to provide special credits to the IMF.
The GAB needs the collective agreement of its members to be activated. Credits are separate from the IMF's normal resources and are for use only by a GAB member facing currency or payments difficulties.
▶ *See also* G10 *and* IMF.

Gamma The measure of change in the delta of an option compared with a price change in the underlying.
▶ *See also* Delta *and* Option.

Gann Angles Specific angles used by technical analysts to draw trendlines from market price tops or bottoms. The most important Gann angle is the 45-degree line because it is seen as the perfect balance between time and price. A major reversal is usually indicated by a break of the 45-degree line.
▶ *See also* Technical Analysis.

Gap A mismatch between a bank's assets and liabilities.

Gapping The process of intentionally mismatching the maturities of assets and liabilities by borrowing short and lending long.

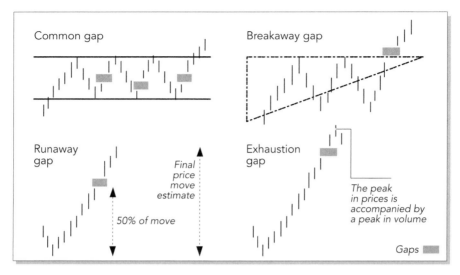

FIGURE 12 Gaps

Gaps Term used by technical analysts to describe the gaps between price levels in charts. Different types of gaps exist. Upside gaps portray market strength and downside gaps show the reverse. The breakaway gap appears at the completion of key price patterns and often signals the start of a significant move.
> *See also* Technical Analysis.

Garman Kohlhagen Model A currency option pricing formula similar to Black & Scholes but with separate conditions for domestic and foreign interest rates.
> *See also* Black & Scholes Model *and* Option.

Gas to Oil Ratio Number of cubic feet of gas per barrel of oil at atmospheric pressure or the volume of gas to volume of oil.

Gateway A network configuration that allows two or more different computer networks to be connected.

GATT General Agreement on Tariffs and Trade. An international agreement among nations to harmonize trade tariffs. Gatt was set up within the World Trade Organisation. ▓ **www.wto.org** ▓
> *See also* WTO.

GDP Gross Domestic Product. Total monetary value of all goods and services produced within a country. GDP does not include income from overseas investments and earnings.
> *See also* GNP.

GDP Deflators Price indices that are applied to value estimates of nominal GDP to produce a more accurate or 'real' value of GDP.
> *See also* GDP.

GDR Global depositary receipts. Depositary receipts issued in more than one country.
  ▷ *See also* ADR.

Gearing The ratio of a company's debt to equity. Gearing is an indicator of a company's ability to service its debt. The higher the proportion of debt to equity, the higher the gearing is said to be. A company with high gearing is more vulnerable to fluctuations in business activity and therefore represents higher risk for equity holders.
  In derivatives markets, gearing is the measure of the amount of cash spent purchasing an option or a futures contract, compared to the actual value of the underlying position.
  Gearing is also known as leverage.
  ▷ *See also* Derivatives.

Geisha Bond A bond privately placed by a non-Japanese borrower in Japan, issued in a currency other than yen.

General Accounting Office Audits US government departments as well as making broader programme evaluations. Headed by the controller general.

General Agreement on Tarfiffs and Trade ▷ *See* GATT.

General Arrangements to Borrow ▷ *See* GAB.

General Obligation Bonds Type of municipal securities issued by US States, counties, special districts, cities, towns and schools.

Gensaki Market Japanese market for medium-term bond financing but also referred to as a repo market. Securities acting as collateral in these operations are both long-term bonds and Treasury bills.

GIF Graphics Interchange Format. Compression format that allows graphical images to be sent easily from one computer to another.

Gilt-edged A term used to describe securities that carry little risk. Government bonds in both the UK and South Africa are known as gilts.

Ginnie Mae Government National Mortgage Association (GNMA). A wholly owned corporate unit of the US Government whose chief function is to guarantee securities backed by pools of federally insured or guaranteed mortgages to aid secondary market liquidity. Its guarantees are known as GNMA pass-through certificates. ■ **www.ginniemae.gov** ■
  ▷ *See also* Securitization.

Given Dealers' language mainly heard through a broker's box when a bid has been hit.

GmbH German company title: abbreviation of Gesellschaft mit beschränkter Haftung, a limited liability company.

GNMA ▷ *See* Ginnie Mae.

GNP Gross National Product. Total value of goods and services produced within an economy including income from overseas investments and earnings.
▶ *See also* GDP.

Go Long/Short ▶ *See* Long *and* Short.

Going Public Term for a privately owned company that seeks a listing on a stock exchange and issues shares to the general public. Also known as a floatation or issuing an IPO.
▶ *See also* Flotation *and* IPO.

Gold Standard A monetary system of fixed exchange rates whose parities were set in relation to gold. Under the system, central banks had to be able to exchange gold for any amount of their currencies. Most developed countries had abandoned the gold standard before the end of the Second World War.

Golden Handcuffs A financial bonus offered to an employee by a company wanting to retain his or her services, usually a manoeuvre that is spread over a number of years.

Golden Hello A financial bonus offered to an employee on joining a company.

Golden Share Exists in various forms but is basically about retaining power if the company is threatened by a takeover. This is typically achieved by vesting the golden share with sufficient voting rights to maintain control and thus fend off potential predators.
▶ *See also* Stock *and* Share.

Good Delivery Delivery of an instrument, in good time, in which all relevant matters – title, endorsement, legal papers and so forth – are in order.

Good Till Cancelled ▶ *See* GTC.

Goodwill The excess price paid for a company over the value of its assets. It is normally only recognized in the accounts of a company when it acquires another business as a going concern for a price that is higher than the book value of its capital and reserves.

Government National Mortgage Association ▶ *See* Ginnie Mae.

Grace Period The time period agreed by the lender whereby the borrower does not start to repay the principal for a number of years although interest payments are made.

Grades Standards set for judging the quality of a commodity.

Grains Wheat, corn (maize), oats, barley, sorghum, rye and millet.

Graphical User Interface ▶ *See* GUI.

Graphics Interchange Format ▶ *See* GIF.

Green Rates Accounting currencies used in assessing payments to farmers within the EU's Common Agricultural Policy (CAP). Under CAP, farmers are paid in agricultural units of account. Green rates were devised to convert these units of account payments into national currencies. They can only be revised by governments, making them far more stable than market rates. The number of green rates was sharply reduced by the introduction of the euro in 1999. Green rates only exist for those countries that remain outside the single currency.

▶ *See also* CAP, European Union *and* Euro.

Greenshoe Option An underwriting agreement provision allowing the issue of additional shares to meet exceptional public demand.

Greenmail In the US, payments by the target of a takeover attempt to the bidder, usually to buy back acquired shares at a premium, with the aim of dissuading the predator from pursuing the bid effort.

Grey Market An informal market in which investors buy and sell securities that have not yet been allotted for settlement after the issue date when the shares become available. These unofficial markets are also described as when issued (W/I).

▶ *See also* W/I.

Gross Domestic Product ▶ *See* GDP.

Gross National Product ▶ *See* GNP.

Gross Price ▶ *See* Dirty Price.

Gross Profit Total profit before deduction of tax and expenses.

Grossing Up An accounting practice calculating the amount of tax needed, in the case of an investment that is subject to tax, to equal the income from an investment that is not subject to tax.

GTC Good Till Cancelled. Limit order that remains valid until ('till') the order is executed or cancelled.

GUI Graphical User Interface. Allows computer developers to build graphical navigation tools such as menus and icons into software.

H

Hacker The term was originally used to describe a sophisticated computer user. However, it has become the label for those users who want to gain unauthorized access to computer systems usually with the intention of doing some harm.

Haircut The difference between the actual market value and the value ascribed to the collateral used in a repo transaction.

▶ *See also* Repurchase Agreement.

Handle ▶ *See* Big Figure.

Hang Seng The Hang Seng Index (HIS) is the benchmark equity index for the Hong Kong Stock Exchange. The index is based on 33 blue-chip stocks, representing 70 per cent of the HKSE's turnover. ▦ **www.hangseng.com** ▦

Hard Currency A currency that can be traded and exchanged, and in which there is a general wide-ranging confidence.

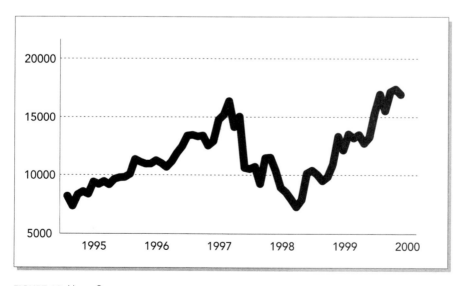

FIGURE 13 Hang Seng

Head and Shoulders Used in technical analysis, head and shoulders patterns are considered to be one of the most reliable of all major reversal patterns. The pattern consists of a major rally (the head) separating two smaller, though not necessarily identical, rallies (the shoulders).

A neckline can be drawn connecting the bottom of the two shoulders and confirmation is normally accepted on a decisive close below that neckline. The inverse head and shoulders is a mirror image of the head and shoulders.

▶ *See also* Technical Analysis.

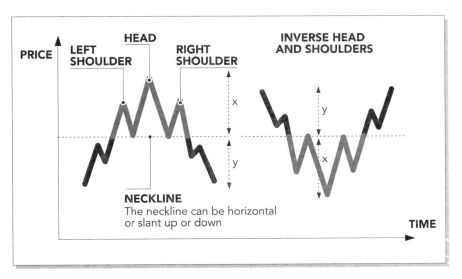

FIGURE 14 Head and Shoulders

Heating Oil A fuel widely used in homes and light industry for heating and is cheaper than gasoline since it is produced from the 'middle cut' of a barrel of crude. Heating oil prices are principally driven by seasonal factors. Also known as gas oil.

Heaven and Hell Bonds Bonds whose redemption value is linked at maturity time to the spot exchange rate of another currency against the denominated currency of the bond. Proceeds from the redemption can take any value between 5 and 200 per cent of the face value.

A variation of a heaven and hell bond is the purgatory and hell bond in which the proceeds from redemption are tied to another spot rate.

Hedge Funds Funds that pursue highly speculative investment strategies, usually using borrowed funds to do so. Thus their balance sheets are highly leveraged. Investors in hedge funds are usually either high net worth individuals prepared to take high risks with their investment for the prospect of very high returns, or large institutional funds investing small proportions of their total assets in speculative ventures.

▶ *See also* Leverage.

Hedging An action or strategy designed to minimize risk. A hedge often takes the form of a transaction in one market or asset, which protects against losses in another – e.g. a company buys an FX (foreign exchange) option to protect against the risk to its business of fluctuations in spot currency rates. Those pursuing hedging strategies are known as hedgers.

▶ *See also* Speculator.

Hermes Hermes Kreditversicherungs Ag. German state export insurance agency.

Herstatt Risk Risk that when dealing with an overseas client or counterparty, the principal may not be recoverable if the counterparty defaults on its payment obligation.

Also called cross-currency settlement risk, but often called the Herstatt risk after the failure of the German bank Bankhaus Herstatt in 1974.

High Low Open Close These represent the four most important types of price information which are displayed in most price displays and charts.

High is the highest level at which a security or commodity has traded, while low is the lowest level. Depending on the instrument, it can be the high/low that day, that year or since price records began. Open/close are the opening and closing levels for any of those periods.

Technical analysts maintain that to understand the market, these prices are the only four pieces of information you really need.

High Tech Stock Term used to describe the stock of companies involved in computer technology and advanced electronics.

Historical Cost The original cost of a company's assets as distinct from replacement cost.

Historical Volatility A measure of volatility based on past price or yield behaviour.

▶ *See also* Volatility.

Hits Each time a user visits a particular web page 'a hit' is registered.

Holder of Record The name of the owner of a security as recorded in the issuing company's records.

Holding Company A company that has control of one or more other companies, often by having a majority of the shares in each subsidiary. Control is usually over areas such as marketing and financial and not investment.

Horizontal Spread An option strategy that involves buying and selling contracts with the same strike price but different maturities, in view of expected moves in volatility. Also known as a calendar spread.

▶ *See also* Option.

Hostile Bid A bid for a company that is not supported by the senior management of that company.

Hot stock A stock whose price suddenly rises or falls sharply.

HTML Hypertext Mark-up Language. The computer language used to create web documents.

HTTP Hypertext Transfer Protocol. An Internet protocol that defines how messages are transmitted and received.

Hydrocarbons Compounds of hydrogen and carbon. Can be found as solids, liquids or gas. Used as a synonym for petroleum.

Hydrocracking Refining technique for converting residual petroleum liquids into high octane gasoline, jet fuels and fuel oils.

Hyperinflation Galloping, self-fuelling inflation, which may trigger an economic collapse.

Hyperlink A link within a document or website that takes the user to another document or site.

Hypertext Mark-up Language ▶ *See* HTML.

Hypertext Transfer Protocol ▶ *See* HTTP.

I

IADB Inter-American Development Bank. The IADB promotes economic and social projects in developing countries with financial and technical assistance and via loans. ▨ www.iadb.org ▨

ICC International Chamber of Commerce. The ICC groups chambers of commerce, business and banking associations from around the world. It has an arbitration court used for settling international business disputes. ▨ www.iccwbo.org ▨

ICCO The International Cocoa Organization. An industry organization that acts as a forum for discussions between cocoa producers and consumers. ▨ www.icco.org ▨

ICO The International Coffee Organization. A forum for discussions between coffee importing and exporting nations. ▨ www.ico.org ▨

IDA International Development Association. An affiliate of the World Bank, which finances development projects and programmes on concessional terms in the poorest countries. ▨ www.worldbank.org/ida/ ▨
   ▶ See also World Bank.

IDB Inter-dealer broker. A broker who acts on behalf of market makers.

IEA International Energy Agency. Set up by the OECD to monitor oil supply and demand, and to supervise consumer levels of oil stocks. ▨ www.iea.org ▨
   ▶ See also OECD.

IFC International Finance Corporation. An affiliate of the World Bank, which helps private enterprises in developing nations and mobilizes domestic and foreign capital, including its own, for this purpose. ▨ www.ifc.org ▨
   ▶ See also World Bank.

ILO International Labour Organization. A UN-sponsored body that is concerned with labour issues.

Illiquid Markets or instruments are described as being illiquid if there is a shortage of buyers or sellers. This shortage means it is also difficult to find a true price for an illiquid security. The opposite of liquid.
   ▶ See also Liquid.

IMF International Monetary Fund. A specialized agency that provides funds to member countries with balance of payments problems under certain conditions of need and strict policy commitments.

The IMF has a wide-ranging brief to oversee the international monetary system, promote exchange rate stability and international trade. It was established by the Bretton Woods Agreement on a system of differential quota subscriptions representing drawing rights and voting powers. Subscriptions come from its member countries. ■ **www.imf.org** ■

► *See also* Bretton Woods.

IMM The International Monetary Market. A division of the Chicago Mercantile Exchange.

► *See also* CME.

Implied volatility The volatility implied in the price of an option. It is a measure of how much the market thinks prices will move given a known option price but does not indicate the direction of the movement expected. Volatility is expressed as an annualized percentage.

► *See also* Volatility.

IMRO The Investment Management Regulatory Organization. The UK authority responsible for regulating the fund management industry.

■ **www.imro.co.uk** ■

In strike The designated point when a trigger option, such as a down and in or an up and in, turns into a conventional option.

In the Money An option is described as being in the money when the current price of the underlying is above the strike or exercise price for a call, and below the strike price for a put.

Options can also be described as being deep in the money when they are likely to expire in the money.

► *See also* Out of the Money *and* At the Money.

Inc Incorporation, a US and Canadian company title. Incorporation is the process by which a company receives a charter and is allowed to operate as a corporation. This process must be recognized in the legal name, i.e. Inc.

Income Money earned from investments, earnings or employment.

Income statement ► *See* Profit and Loss Account.

Income stock ► *See* Blue Chip Stock.

Incomes policy Broad term covering various direct forms of inflation control by a government. Can include a freeze or limitation on increases in prices, wages, dividends, investment income and rents.

Independent A non-integrated oil company usually active in only one or two sectors of the industry.

Independent Petroleum Exporting Countries ► *See* IPEC.

Index A composite of values that is designed to measure change in a market or an economy.

Indexing Creating a portfolio such that its weighting recreates and matches the performance of a broad-based index. Investment funds constructed in such a manner are known as index funds.

Index-linked Bonds Bonds in which the coupons are linked to a retail or consumer price index.

Index Tracking A process whereby a fund manager aims to reproduce the performance of a stock market index. A manager buys the shares that make up the index in the relevant proportions in which they are represented in the index.

Indications of Interest ▶ *See* IOI.

Indicators ▶ *See* Economic Indicators.

Indirect Quotation An FX term for the number of units of foreign currency that can be exchanged for one unit of domestic currency. The most common example of an indirect quotation outside the US is the sterling/dollar rate. US banks use indirect quotations in their international dealings but use direct quotations for domestic purposes.

Industrial Production A measure of the output of goods-producing industries, used as an indicator of the state of an economy.

Inflation Inflation exists when the price of a good or service rises persistently. Different types of inflation are defined by their cause. Demand-pull inflation is caused by excess demand in the economy, while cost-push inflation is caused by high costs.
    ▶ *See also* Hyperinflation *and* Stagflation.

Inflation Risk The risk associated with the return from an investment not being offset by the loss in purchasing power caused by inflation.

Initial Margin The margin payment paid to a clearing house by both the buyer and the seller of a futures contract to protect against potential losses.
    ▶ *See also* Clearing House *and* Margin.

Initial Public Offering ▶ *See* IPO.

Inland Revenue The UK government department responsible for collecting tax.

Inland Revenue Service ▶ *See* IRS.

INSEE Institut National de la Statistique et des Études Économiques (French National Statistics Institute). Collates and issues a number of government economic indicators. ▪ **www.insee.fr** ▪

Insider Trading Exploitation of inside or privileged information for profit in market transactions. This is illegal in many countries.

Insolvency When a company is unable to pay its debts as and when they fall due. A company is also insolvent when its liabilities, including contingent and prospective liabilities, exceed the value of the assets. Opposite of solvency.
    ▶ *See also* Solvency.

Institutional Investors Financial institutions, such as pensions funds and investment trusts, which invest large amounts of capital in financial markets on behalf of their clients.

Intangibles ▶ *See* Assets/Liabilities.

Integrated Oil Company One that undertakes all principal oil industry functions – exploration, production, transportation, refining and marketing.

Integrated Producer A producer that owns mines, smelters and refineries and, in some cases, fabricating plants.

Integrated Services Digital Network ▶ *See* ISDN.

Inter-American Development Bank ▶ *See* IADB.

Inter-Dealer Broker ▶ *See* IDB.

Interbank Market Term used to describe professional markets between banks, most commonly used to refer to the wholesale market in foreign exchange.

Interest Bearing Term used to describe instruments that pay a given rate of interest on the principal amount, either in one payment, typically at maturity, or as a series of payments over the life. Also referred to as coupon bearing.

Interest Cover Interest cover, or income earning, expresses how many times a company's interest obligations could be met out of gross profits. It is calculated by dividing a company's pre-tax operating income by its interest obligations, for a given period.

Interest Rate The cost, often annual, paid by a borrower to a lender over a period of time. It is intended to compensate a lender for the sacrifice of losing immediate use of money, for the inflationary erosion of its buying power over the life of the loan and for the risk involved in lending.
The rate of interest is a price that can be analyzed in the normal framework of demand and supply analysis.

Interest Rate Differential The difference in yield between two comparable instruments denominated in different currencies. Used in forward foreign exchange pricing.

Interest Rate Risk The potential for losses or reduced income arising from adverse moves in interest rates.

Interest Rate Swap ▶ *See* Swap.

Interim Dividend Dividend paid by a company in a trading period, usually half yearly but can be quarterly. Authorized solely by the board of directors subject to shareholder approval.
▶ *See also* Dividend.

Internal Rate of Return ▶ *See* IRR.

International Accounting Standards Committee An international committee that formulates and publishes accounting standards. Members comprise over 100 national accounting bodies. ▧ **www.iasc.org.uk** ▧

International Bank for Reconstruction and Development ▷ *See* World Bank.

International Chamber of Commerce ▷ *See* ICC.

International Cocoa Organization ▷ *See* ICCO.

International Coffee Organization ▷ *See* ICO.

International Development Association ▷ *See* IDA.

International Energy Agency ▷ *See* IEA.

International Finance Corporation ▷ *See* IFC.

International Labour Organization ▷ *See* ILO.

International Monetary Fund ▷ *See* IMF.

International Monetary Market ▷ *See* IMM.

International Organization of Securities Commissions ▷ *See* IOSCO.

International Petroleum Exchange ▷ *See* IPE.

International Securities Market Association ▷ *See* ISMA.

International Share Offering Occurs when shares of a domestic company are sold internationally via a syndicate of underwriters. They can be either new shares or a secondary offering.

International Sugar Organization Group that brings together sugar-importing and exporting countries. ▧ **www.isosugar.org** ▧

International Swap and Derivatives Association ▷ *See* ISDA.

International Wheat Council Group that brings together wheat-producing and consuming countries.

Internet A global computer network that allows users to publish and access a wide variety of data and information in web format.

Internet Service Provider ▷ *See* ISP.

Interpolation The process of determining a rate (or other variable) that lies between a series of known rates. Three types of interpolation exist: linear, logarithmic and cubic.

>   ▷ *See also* Extrapolation.

Intervention The market participation of a central bank to influence monetary conditions. The most common intervention is seen in the currency markets, when the bank or banks may simply be seeking to stabilize exchange rates rather than to steer them to any particular level.

>   ▷ *See also* Concerted Intervention.

Intraday A term that means 'within the day' and usually refers to prices in financial markets. An intraday price can be any price between the opening and the close. Common intraday intervals used to record price changes include tick, five-minute, half-hourly and hourly.

Intraday Limit Limit allowed on a dealer's position in each and all currencies during the course of the trading day.

Intranet A secure internal network used by an organization to publish information to its employees.
> *See also* Extranet.

Intrinsic Value When an option is in the money it is said to have intrinsic value. It is calculated by taking the difference between the forward market value of the underlying instrument and the strike price of the option.
> *See also* In the Money *and* Option.

Introduction An introduction involves the listing of existing shares on a stock exchange. No new capital is raised and there is no transfer of ownership.

Investment Bank A US term used to describe banks that specialize in financial market activities rather than lending and money transmission.

Investment Fund Funds that manage portfolios of money. There are basically two types of investment funds – open-ended mutual funds, which are also known as unit trusts, and closed-end publicly quoted funds, which are known as investment trusts.

Investment Grade Bonds that carry credit ratings of BBB/Baa or above by the credit rating agencies and are considered to be safe investments. The agencies do not anticipate that the issuers are likely to default at the time the rating is issued.
> *See also* Junk Bonds.

Invisible Supply Stocks – notably commodities – outside commercial channels whose exact quantity cannot be identified, but which in theory are available to the market.

Invisibles International transactions in services as opposed to trade in physical goods or merchandise. They form part of the current account balance of payments and include funds arising from shipping, tourism, insurance, banking and commodity services.

IOI Indications of Interest. An IOI represents an investor's interest in purchasing securities, which have not yet been issued.

IOSCO International Organization of Securities Commissions. An organization comprising the securities administrations from more than 50 countries. Seeks to develop securities markets and observance of securities regulations.
> **www.iosco.org**

IP Address An IP address is the unique number that identifies each computer on a network.

IPE The International Petroleum Exchange. Europe's leading market for energy derivatives and the home of the Brent futures contract. ▪ **www.ipe.uk.com** ▪
▸ *See also* Brent.

IPO Initial Public Offering. The first offering of shares to the public by a privately owned company. Used by companies to raise new funds or achieve a listing on an exchange. The issuer normally offers to the public through an underwriter who sets the price and promotes the offering.
Also known as a flotation or going public.
▸ *See also* Flotation *and* Going Public.

IPEC The Independent Petroleum Exporting Countries. An informal group of oil exporters who do not belong to the Organization of Petroleum Exporting Countries.
▸ *See also* OPEC.

IRR Internal rate of return. A measure of return that takes both the size and timing of cash flows into account. The formula is identical in structure to that which is used to calculate the yield to maturity of a bond.

IRS Inland Revenue Service. The US federal agency responsible for the collection of taxes. ▪ **www.irs.gov** ▪

I/S Danish and Norwegian company title: abbreviation of Interessentskab.

ISDA The International Swap and Derivatives Association. An international trade organization for the OTC derivatives markets. ISDA acts as a forum to discuss industry issues and promotes best practices within the derivatives business.
▪ **www.isda.org** ▪

ISDN Integrated Services Digital Network. A high-technology telecommunications network that allows data to be transferred over phone lines as digital signals, allowing much higher transfer rates.

Islamic Development Bank An international bank that encourages economic and social development in its 53 member nations and of Muslim communities in non-member countries following Islamic law. ▪ **www.isdb.org** ▪

ISMA International Securities Market Association. A self-regulatory body and trade association for the securities industry. ISMA was originally set up as the Association of International Bond Dealers with a remit of establishing a structure for the eurobond market.
▪ **www.isam.co.uk** ▪

ISP Internet Service Provider. Remote computer networks that connect users to the Internet.

Issue Date ▸ *See* Dated Date.

Issued Capital/Share Capital Share capital that has actually been issued – that is allotted – to shareholders, as opposed to authorized share capital, which is the maximum amount of share capital that a company is allowed to issue by its constitution or charter.

Issue Price Price at which securities are sold on issue. This can be at face value or par, at a discount or at a premium.

IT Information technology.

J

Java A programming language developed by Sun Microsystems to create self-running applications.

J Curve An expression to describe the reaction of the balance of trade following a devaluation. The trade balance deteriorates as import costs rise, then recovers to surplus as exports expand in volume due to cheaper exchange costs.

JD Slovenian company title: abbreviation of Javna Druzba.

JPEG Joint Photographic Experts Group. A file format used to store and transfer graphical images electronically.

Junk Bonds High-yield bonds, which are rated below investment grade by credit agencies. Also known as speculative grade bonds.

> *See also* Investment Grade.

K

Kairi In technical analysis, this indicator charts the percentage difference between the current closing value and its simple moving average. Can be used either as a trend indicator or as an overbought/oversold signal.
> *See also* Overbought, Oversold *and* Technical Analysis.

Kampo The Postal Insurance Bureau of the Japanese Posts and Telecommunications Ministry. It is one of the major Japanese institutional investors in foreign bonds and foreign exchange markets.

Kassen ▶ *See also* Bundeskassenobligationen (BOBL).

Kassenverein The Central Depository Bank for Securities. The clearing agent of the German Stock Exchange.

Keidanren A forum that comprises Japan's leading industry and business figures.

Kerb Market In financial markets the term kerb is used to describe trading outside official market hours. The expression comes from trading literally taking place on the kerb outside the stock exchange.

Keynsian Economics Economic theories developed by John Maynard Keynes based on a cause and effect analysis of variations in aggregate spending and income. These theories opposed the free market philosophy and argued that economic performance could be improved by government intervention.

Kft Hungarian company title: abbreviation of Korlatolt felelossegu tarsasag.

KG German and Swiss company title: abbreviation of Kommanditgessellschaft and Kollectivgessellschaft respectively.

Kicker An added feature of a debt obligation designed to enhance marketability.

KK Japanese company title: abbreviation of Kabushiki Kaisha.

Kkt Hungarian company title: abbreviation of Kozkereseti tarasag.

KmG Swiss company title: abbreviation of Kommanditgessellschaft.

K/S Danish company title: abbreviation of Kommanditselskab.

Knockout Option A type of barrier option.
> *See also* Barrier Option.

L

Labour Market The market for jobs comprised of workers searching for work and employers offering work.

LAN Local area network. A computer network that links users in a small area such as the same building.

Ladder Option An option on which the strike price can be moved to a more favourable level when the original strike price is reached or overtaken by the spot rate.

▶ *See also* Option.

Lagging/Leading Indicators Lagging indicators are economic indicators that follow a change in the economic cycle. Leading indicators precede, and consequently are used to predict, changes in economic cycles.

▶ *See also* Economic Indicators.

Lambda The measurement of the leverage of an option, showing the relationship between a percentage change in the price of the underlying and a percentage change in the option premium.

▶ *See also* Option.

Last Notice Day Final day for the issuing of notices of intent to deliver against a futures contract.

▶ *See also* Futures.

Last Trading Day Last day for trading in the current delivery month. Futures contracts outstanding at the end of the last trading day must be settled by delivery of the underlying asset or by cash settlement.

▶ *See also* Cash Settlement *and* Futures.

Laundering The covert action of passing money through channels secretively or via a chain of financial transactions to evade detection often using offshore facilities.

LBMA London Bullion Market Association. A trade association for precious metals traders. ■ **www.lbma.org** ■

L/C Letter of Credit. A letter of credit is a guarantee by a bank on behalf of its corporate customer that a payment will be made if contractual obligations are met. Letters of credit can be traded on the secondary market.

▶ *See also* Secondary Market.

LCE The London Commodity Exchange. Europe's leading market for the trading of soft commodity futures and options. The LCE was merged with LIFFE in 1996.
▶ *See also* LIFFE.

Lda Portuguese, Brazilian and Spanish company title: abbreviation of Limitada.

LDC Lesser (or less) developed country. A term that was used to describe developing countries where the economy was primarily based on agriculture and industry contributed less than 10 per cent of GDP. LDC has been replaced by the more widely defined term emerging markets.
▶ *See also* Emerging Markets.

Lead Manager/Underwriter The institution awarded the mandate by a borrower to raise money via a bond or loan. The lead manager guarantees the liquidity of the deal, arranges the syndication of the issue and undertakes a major underwriting and distribution commitment. The lead manager forms a syndicate of co-lead managers, co-managers and underwriters.
▶ *See also* Mandate.

Leads and Lags Accelerated and decelerated foreign trade payments and receipts, usually associated with exchange rate speculation. In anticipation of a devaluation, payments for exports are delayed while an importer accelerates his payments.

LEAPS Long-term equity anticipation securities. Long-term options on individual stocks with an expiry date of up to two years.

Lender of Last Resort One of the main functions of a central bank, which steps in to lend money to troubled financial institutions if they cannot find any other means of raising funds.
▶ *See also* Central Bank.

Lending Margin The fixed spread that borrowers agree to pay above an agreed base of interest.

Letter of Credit ▶ *See* L/C.

Letter Stock A type of ordinary privately-issued share in the US, which is therefore not registered with the SEC. These shares are not easy to transfer.
▶ *See also* SEC.

Leverage ▶ *See* Gearing.

Leveraged Buyout Funds are raised to take over a company and that company's assets are used as collateral (or as leverage) for the borrowing. The purchaser then repays the loans out of the acquired company's cash flow, or by selling its assets.

Liabilities Liabilities arise from borrowings and credits used to finance assets.
▶ *See also* Assets.

Liability Management ▶ *See* Asset Management.

LIBID The London Interbank Bid Rate/The rate at which banks take deposits from each other.

LIBOR The London Interbank Offered Rate. The rate at which banks are prepared to lend money market funds to each other. LIBOR is a key interest rate level used for setting rates on loans and floating rate notes.

Licensed Warehouse Warehouse approved by an exchange from which a commodity may be delivered under a futures contract.
▶ *See also* Futures.

Lien The right to take assets to cover an unpaid debt.

LIFFE The London International Financial Futures and Options Exchange. Europe's leading market for short-term interest rate futures. The LCE and London Trading Options Market merged with LIFFE bringing futures and options trading in soft commodities and equity options under the exchange's umbrella.
▓ **www.liffe.com** ▓

LIMEAN The London interbank mean price.

Limit Order An order stipulating the price at which it can be executed. The maximum price is stipulated for a buy order and the minimum for a sell. Limit orders are normally valid until a certain time specified by the counterparty or GTC.
▶ *See also* GTC.

Limit Up/Down The maximum advance and decline from a previous day's settlement price allowed in one trading session are known as limit up and limit down. Some markets do not trade again during the session after a limit up/down move unless prices fall (or rise). Other markets suspend trading temporarily when limits are hit and then reopen with expanded limit levels.
▶ *See also* Circuit Breakers.

Limited Liability A restriction of the owner's loss in the business to the amount of capital invested.

Line Chart Used in technical analysis. A line chart is the simplest form of chart. It is a plain record of a price charted against time with the changes marked as dots and conjoined in a determining line.
▶ *See also* Technical Analysis.

Liquid Markets or instruments are described as being liquid, and having depth, if there are enough buyers and sellers to absorb sudden shifts in supply and demand without price distortions. The opposite of illiquid.
▶ *See also* Illiquid.

Liquidity Margin A liquidity margin is a good faith performance guarantee. In repurchase agreements, lenders often seek such a margin from borrowers perhaps by receiving securities in excess of the money borrowed.

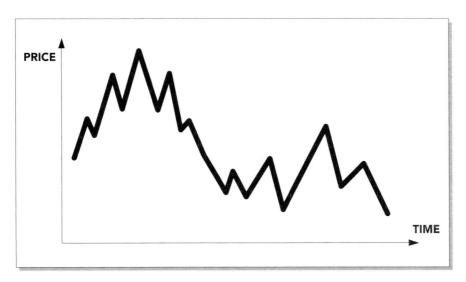

FIGURE 15 Line Chart

Liquidity Risk The risk a dealer has of not being able to unwind a position or enter into a position at a desired point of time.

Listed Stock A security that is listed on a stock exchange and can therefore be traded in the market.

Listing Requirements Required by a stock exchange before a stock is listed and ready to trade. Each exchange sets its own listing requirements and criteria include considerations such as the number of publicly-held shares and number of shareholders.

LLC US company title: abbreviation of limited liability company.

Lloyd's An insurance market based in London that specializes in marine insurance. Capital is provided by a number of members known as 'names'.

LLP US company title: abbreviation of limited liability partnership.

LME London Metal Exchange. Europe's leading market for trading in metals futures and options. The LME acts as an international barometer of supply and demand for metals worldwide and its official prices are used by producers and consumers for their long-term contacts. ▓ **www.lme.co.uk** ▓

LNG Liquefied natural gas. Natural gas that has been liquefied by refrigeration or pressure to facilitate storage or transport. Generally consists of methane.

Load A premium charged by some funds at either purchase or sale, to cover the fund's expenses.

Loan Loss Provisions Funds set aside to cover anticipated loan losses, which appear on a bank's income statement as an operating expense.

Local Area Network ▷ *See* LAN.

Locals Individual traders operating on futures or options exchanges purely for their own account.

Loco The cost of goods where they lie. In gold trading the price is quoted for delivery to a certain location.

London Bullion Market Association ▷ *See* LBMA.

London Club An informal group of commercial banks which negotiates with debtor nations that have loan problems.
▷ *See also* Paris Club.

London Commondity Exchange ▷ *See* LCE.

London International Financial Futures and Options Exchange ▷ *See* LIFFE.

London Metal Exchange ▷ *See* LME.

London Stock Exchange ▷ *See* LSE.

Long Investors are described as 'long' when they have bought assets in the hope that prices will rise and that they can sell them when prices have peaked. The opposite of short.
▷ *See also* Short.

Long Bond Commonly used name for the 30-year US Treasury bond.

Long Dated Forwards Forward foreign exchange contracts with value dates beyond 12 months.
▷ *See also* Forwards.

Long Hedge The purchase of a Futures or option position to protect against a price rise in the corresponding cash market. Opposite to short hedge.
▷ *See also* Hedging.

Long Position A position showing a purchase or a greater number of purchases than sales in anticipation of a rise in prices. A long position can be closed out through the sale of an equivalent amount.
▷ *See also* Short Position.

Long Ton A ton of 2,240 pounds weight, equal to 1.016 metric tonnes.

Lookback/Forward Option An option that grants the holder the retroactive right to set the strike at the lowest price (on a call) or at the highest price (on a put) reached by the underlying within the lookback period.
▷ *See also* Option.

Loss Limit The maximum loss permitted on a position before the dealer is required to cut losses and square or reduce the position.

Louvre Accord An agreement on currency stability in 1987 by the finance ministers of the Group of Five Nations and Canada following the prolonged fall in the US dollar after the Plaza Agreement.

LP US company title: abbreviation of limited partnership.

LPG Liquefied petroleum gas. Light hydrocarbons from oil-bearing strata, which are gaseous at normal temperatures, but which are liquefied by refrigeration or pressure to facilitate storage or transport. Mainly propane and butane.

LSE London Stock Exchange ▨ **www.londonstockexchange.com** ▨

Ltd UK company title: abbreviation of Limited. Generally replaced by public limited company or plc. Also used for quoted companies in Australia, Canada and New Zealand.

Ltée French Canadian company title: abbreviation of Limitée.

M&A Mergers and acquisitions.

Maastricht Treaty Agreed in December 1991 by the 12 member nations of the then European Community, which set the timetable and criteria for Economic and Monetary Union within the bloc. The treaty also created a new entity to replace the EC, the European Union, with new political and social responsibilities. It is also known as the Treaty on European Union.

▶ *See also* EMU *and* EU.

Macauley duration ▶ *See* Duration.

MACD Moving Average Covergence/Divergence. This technical analysis tool uses two exponential moving averages to produce two lines, which oscillate above and below a zero line. Sell and buy signals are generated when the lines cross. Overbought and oversold signals can be indicated when both lines are significantly above or below the zero line respectively.

▶ *See also* Technical Analysis.

Macro-economics Study of aggregate economic behaviour such as total output, economic growth, inflation and unemployment.

▶ *See also* Economic Indicators.

Maintenance Call ▶ *See* Margin Call.

Maintenance Margin The lowest balance of funds that a clearing house or brokerage firm will allow a counterparty when trading on margin.

▶ *See also* Margin *and* Margin Trading.

Majority Interest A major equity interest comprising more than half the shares in a company.

Majority Rule In technical analysis, this indicator calculates the percentage of the last specified periods during which an instrument had rising values. This analysis may be used either as a trend-following device or as an overbought/oversold indicator.

▶ *See also* Technical Analysis.

Majors Multinational oil companies, which by virtue of size, age and/or degree of integration, are among the pre-eminent firms in the international petroleum industry.

Managed Currency A currency is described as managed if the government exerts some influence over the exchange rate and the rate is not determined purely by free market forces.

Managed Float ▶ *See* Dirty Float.

Management Buyout ▶ *See* MBO.

Management Group Group of financial institutions that co-ordinates closely with the lead manager in the distribution and pricing of an issue.

Mandate The authority from a borrower to the lead manager to proceed with a loan or bond issue on the terms agreed.

Margin Margin is the collateral paid to cover, at least in part, contractual obligations and protect against potential unlimited loss potential.
Initial margin is the payment required by a clearing house from both the buyer and seller of a futures contract.
To ensure that margin requirements keep pace with subsequent market movements, variation margin is also called for. This is calculated by revaluing all positions with reference to the closing prices each day.
▶ *See also* Initial Margin, Mark to Market, Margin Trading *and* Variation Margin.

Margin Account An account enabling an investor to trade without having the full amount of funds available.
▶ *See also* Margin *and* Margin Trading.

Margin Call A call made by the clearing house or broker to a counterparty whose margin account has fallen below the minimum requirement or the maintenance margin. Also referred to as a maintenance call.
▶ *See also* Maintenance Margin.

Margin Trading An investor pays a certain amount of cash to fund a transaction and borrows the remainder from a broker at some rate of interest. Margin trading provides gearing to investors since their small amount of funds goes a lot further when combined with additional funds.

Mark to Market The process by which a position or portfolio is revalued based on the day's closing price, thereby reflecting the unrealized profit and loss.

Markdown The amount or percentage deducted from the bid price when a customer sells to a broker or market maker in the OTC market, which is regarded as a type of commission. Also used to describe market makers adjusting their prices down to reflect changing market conditions. Opposite of markup.
▶ *See also* Markup.

Market Capitalization Total value of a company's securities at current prices as quoted on a stock exchange. Market capitalization is calculated by multiplying the total number of shares by the market price. Also, can denote the total value of the whole of a stock exchange's securities or of one sector of its securities.

Market Economy An economy where demand and supply in free markets determine the allocation of resources. However, most countries impose some limitations within this economic system.

Market If Touched ▶ *See* MIT.

Market Maker Individual or firm that stands ready to trade in one or more securities at quoted bid and ask prices. Market makers usually hold an inventory of the securities they make markets in.

Market Order An order that should be executed immediately whatever the current price.

Market Risk ▶ *See* Systematic Risk.

Market Trend General direction, ignoring short-term fluctuations, of overall price movements in a market.

Market-value Weighted Index An index in which greater weight is given to shares that have a larger market capitalization, so that they have more influence than shares with a lower market capitalization.
▶ *See also* Market Capitalization.

Markup The amount or percentage added to the offer price when a customer buys from a broker or market maker in the OTC market, which is regarded as a type of commission. Also used to describe market makers adjusting their prices upwards to reflect changing market conditions. Opposite of markdown.
▶ *See also* Markdown.

Master Agreement The initial agreement signed between two parties proposing to enter into swap, which defines all criteria such as references for fixing rates and the status of counterparties.

Matador Bond A bond issued in Spain by a foreign borrower and denominated in pesetas. A type of foreign bond.

Matched Book A book where the maturity dates for a bank or trader's liabilities match those of the assets. Also, where borrowing costs equal the interest earned on investments.

MATIF Marché à Terme International de France. France's financial futures exchange. ■ **www.matif.fr** ■

Maturity The length of time between the issue of a security and date on which it becomes payable in full. Most bonds are issued with a fixed maturity date. Those without one are known as perpetuals.

Maturity Value The amount to be paid back at maturity; in bond trading also called principal.

MBO Management Buyout. Purchase by the managers of a company of part or all of its shares to set it up as an independent concern. The managers act as principals and usually do not provide all the financing.

MBS Mortgage-backed Security. A security backed by, or secured by, a pool or package of mortgage loans. Monthly payments of principal and interest from the underlying pool of mortgages is passed along to the holder of the security.
▶ *See also* Securitization.

M-commerce A form of e-commerce used to describe the buying and selling of goods over mobile phones.
▶ *See also* E-commerce.

Mean Calculated by taking the sum of a set of values and then dividing that figure by the total number of values. Also known as the average.

Median The middle-ranking value of a set of values laid out in numerical order.

Medium-term Notes ▶ *See* MTN.

Merchant Bank ▶ *See* Investment Bank.

MERCOSUR Mercado Común del Sur (Southern Common Market). A Latin American trade bloc that aims to promote free trade and co-operation between its members. Argentina, Brazil, Paraguay and Uruguay were founding members, Chile and Bolivia are associate members.
▪ **www.mercosur.org** ▪

Merger A fusion of two or more companies. Can also represent an acquisition or takeover.

Metric Ton 2,204.6223 pounds in weight or 1,000 kilogrammes.

Mezzanine Finance A type of second-tier funding capital midway between debt and equity in that it offers a higher interest rate than senior debt but provides a lower longer-term return than equity. This allows large deals to be structured in the most suitable method for investors and lenders. Often used in management buyouts.

Mibtel The Mibtel index is the benchmark all-share index for the Italian stock market. The MIB 30 is the Milan blue-chip index. ▪ **www.mibtel.it** ▪

Micro-economics Study of the economic action of individual firms and small well-defined groupings of individuals and sectors.
▶ *See also* Macro-economics.

Middle Office The part of an institution's settlement process that most closely liaises with the front office, inputting trades and reporting positions.
▶ *See also* Front Office *and* Back Office.

MIF The Mercato Italiano Futures. Italy's financial futures market.

Mine Dealers' language. The dealer takes the offer that has been quoted by his counterparty. It has to be qualified by the amount. Confirms the act of purchasing.

Minimum Price Movement The smallest unit of change possible in the futures contract price.
▶ *See also* Tick.

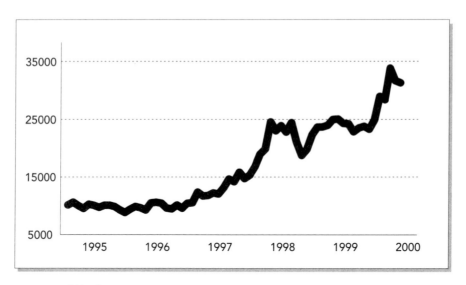

FIGURE 16 Mibtel

Minority Interest The share of a parent company's net profits taken by the minority shareholders in partially-owned subsidiaries.

Mismatch A difference in maturities of funds borrowed and funds invested. A mismatched book occurs when short and long positions do not complement each other.
▶ *See also* Matched Book.

Mismatch Note A note on which coupon refixes and the reference rate are mismatched with one another, e.g. a note refixing against six-month LIBOR on a monthly basis.
▶ *See also* LIBOR.

MIT Market If Touched. Written as MIT. An order to sell or buy at a specific price if the market reaches that price.

Mixed Economy Midway between a planned economy and a market economy. Thus the state runs one or more sectors or parts thereof alongside generally free market activities.
▶ *See also* State Planning.

MMC Monopolies and Mergers Commission. The UK authority responsible for vetting mergers to ensure they do not result in monopolies.
▶ *See also* Monopoly.

Mode The more frequently occurring value within a set of values.

MOFs Multi-option facilities that allow a borrower to obtain funds from various short- or long-term instruments. May include bank advances, commercial paper and euronotes. A variety of currencies can also be available.

Momentum In technical analysis, a type of oscillator that is used to measure the rate of change – as opposed to the actual price level. The momentum indicator is the difference between the price of the instrument today and the price in the previous determined periods. This positive or negative difference is plotted around a zero line. It is used to signal overbought or oversold conditions as well as entry and exit points.

▷ *See also* Technical Analysis.

MONEP Marché des Options Négociables de Paris. The Paris traded options market specializing in stock and index options. ▨ **www.monep.fr** ▨

Monetarism Theory that advocates strict control of money supply as the major weapon of monetary policy, especially against inflation.

Monetary Policy Government policy that deals with total money supply and general level of interest. Governments often delegate monetary policy implementation to central banks.

▷ *See also* Central Banks, Fiscal Policy *and* Money Supply.

Monetary Policy Committee ▷ *See* MPC.

Money Money is a financial asset, a store of wealth and a recognized medium of exchange. Definitions of money and money supply vary from country to country but fall into two categories – broad and narrow.

▷ *See also* Money Supply.

Money Centre Bank A large bank which lends to and borrows from governments, organizations and other banks as opposed to consumers.

Money Flow Index A technical analysis indicator. A volume-weighted relative strength index which attempts to measure the strength of money entering and leaving the market.

▷ *See also* Technical Analysis *and* Relative Strength Index.

Money Market A wholesale market for the buying and selling of money. Money markets trade in debt instruments with residual maturities of 12 months or less.

Money Market Yield The yield of security expressed under the money market daycount convention, normally measured in basis points.

Money Supply Total stock of money in an economy. Definitions of money supply vary but fall into two categories – broad and narrow.

Moneyback Option An option that compensates the original premium at the expiry date.

▷ *See also* Option.

Monopolies and Mergers Commission ▷ *See* MMC.

Monopoly When a person or organization controls the market for a given product or service.

Moody's A leading credit rating agency. Moody's assessments of the creditworthiness of borrowers are widely watched in the capital markets.
■ **www.moodys.com** ■

Moral Persuasion A term used when central banks and governments aim to influence market participants to do what they wish by persuasion rather than by coercion.

Moratorium The suspension or delay, by the borrower, of principal repayments and possibly interest due, following the need to settle economic, monetary and financial affairs. If it is determined that interest will in fact be paid, then banks can continue to classify the loan as a performing asset.

Mortgage-backed Security ▶ *See* MBS.

Mortgage Pool Mortgages are packaged, or pooled, and securities are issued representing shares in the pool. The mortgages bear the same maturity date and same interest rate on the same class of property.
▶ *See also* Securitization.

Moving Average A technical analysis indicator that provides a way of 'smoothing' out data and which is used to confirm price trends. A moving average is usually created by adding a series of closing prices and then averaging the data on a period-by-period basis. As the period moves on, the oldest price in the sequence is dropped and replaced by the current price.
▶ *See also* Technical Analysis.

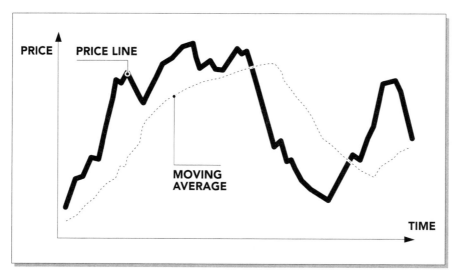

FIGURE 17 Moving average

Most Favoured Nation Undertaking by two countries to give each other the maximum tariff concessions on their mutual trade which they already grant to other countries.

Moving Average Convergence/Divergence ▶ *See* MACD.

Moving Average Crossover Technical analysts interpret crossovers between two moving averages – one using a short interval and the other a longer interval – as significant buy or sell signals.
  ▶ *See also* Moving Average *and* Technical Analysis.

Moving Strike Option An option on which a single strike price is not determined for the life of the option but will vary over time.

MPC The Bank of England's Monetary Policy Committee, the bank's interest-rate setting body.

MSCI Indices The Morgan Stanley Capital International indices. A group of regional, national and industry performance benchmarks designed to help compare world equity markets. Each index is constructed according to a rigorous and consistent methodology. More international equity funds are measured against one of the MSCI indices, including the hallmark EAFE index, than any other index.
  The MSCI indices are calculated using Laspeyere weighted arithmetic averages. ▨ **www.msci.com** ▨
  ▶ *See also* Arithmetic Average *and* Weighted Index.

MTN Medium-term notes. Borrowings out to about five years typically issued under a similar borrowing facility as for commercial paper. MTNs issued in the Euromarkets are known as EMTNs.

MTS Mercato Telematico Secondario. A screen-based system showing two-way prices of Italian Government debt issues by market makers and supervized by the Banca d'Italia.

Multinational A publicly-owned company that operates commercially in a number of countries outside its own base. Usually its activities in each country encompass all aspects of production of its goods or services. Such companies are often listed on more than one stock exchange or have shares available via depositary receipts.
  ▶ *See also* ADR.

Multiples ▶ *See* P/E Ratio.

Multiplier Bond A bond that allows the investor to convert coupons into identical bonds and to reinvest coupons on these subsequent bonds. The borrower gains a cash flow benefit because the payouts are being converted into extra debt. Also known as a bunny bond.

Municipal Notes Short-term US securities, typically out to three years maximum, issued by state and local governments and agencies. Commonly known as munis. Types of municipal note include: tax anticipation notes (TANs); revenue anticipation notes (RANs); grant anticipation notes (GANs); bond anticipation notes (BANs); tax exempt commercial paper.

Mutual Fund/Unit Trust An open-ended investment trust or unit trust, which pools together funds from many investors to establish a diversified portfolio of investments. After the initial public offering, it continuously sells and redeems its shares while investing the combined contributions from the public at large in various securities and paying them dividends in proportion to their holdings.

▶ *See also* Investment fund.

NAFTA North American Free Trade Agreement, a three-member free trade zone between the US, Canada and Mexico. **www.nafta-sec-alena.org**

Naked Position A long or short position that has not been hedged.

Naked Warrant Issued as a stand-alone warrant instead of being attached to a bond. Issuers save costs because the warrant exercise period corresponds to the call feature of a previous bond issue so a call premium need not be paid.

NAPM National Association of Purchasing Management. This US association produces a monthly index on business activity, which is widely watched by financial markets. **www.napm.org**

NASD National Association of Securities Dealers. A US organization for brokers and dealers that formulates legal and ethical standards of conduct for its members. **www.nasd.com**

NASDAQ The National Association of Securities Dealers' Automated Quotations System, owned and operated by the National Association of Securities Dealers (NASD). NASDAQ is an electronic stock market based in New York listing many leading high-tech companies. The exchange's index – the NASDAQ Composite – has become an alternative benchmark to the DJIA. **www.nasdaq.com**
▶ *See also* High Tech Stock *and* DJIA.

National Accounts The national accounts are the official income account, cash flow statement and balance sheet for the economy of a country. These accounts give a comprehensive analysis of GDP and its components, and include detailed financial accounts related to the government, company, household and foreign trade sectors.

National Association of Purchasing Management ▶ *See* NAPM.

National Association of Securities Dealers ▶ *See* NASD.

National Association of Securities Dealers' Automated Quotations System ▶ *See* NASDAQ.

National Debt Total indebtedness of a government as a result of cumulative net budget deficits. Normally financed by the sale of government securities and debt instruments.

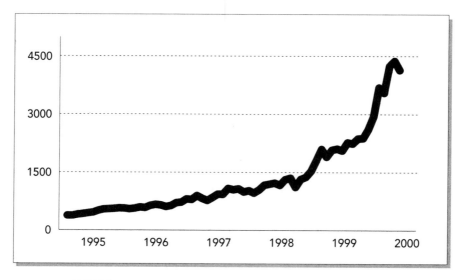

FIGURE 18 NASDAQ

Natural Gas Liquids Consist of natural gas, liquid petroleum gases and natural gasoline.

Natural Gasoline A light liquid hydrocarbon mixture that is recovered from natural gas. It is similar to motor gasoline but has a lower octane number.

Nautical Mile Varies from 6,045.93 feet on the equator to 6,107.98 feet in latitude 90 degrees. A mean nautical mile is 6,076.91 feet.

Navigator Bonds Bonds issued by foreign borrowers in escudos in Portugal. Usually listed in Luxembourg as well as Lisbon.

Near Money Assets, such as money market fund shares, bank time deposits and government securities, which are readily convertible into cash. This also applies to bonds near their redemption date.

Nearbys Nearest delivery months of a futures contract.

Negative Carry Where the financing cost of a position is greater than the return.

Negative Pledge Clause in a bond agreement which prevents the borrower from pledging greater security or collateral to other lenders.

Negative Stock Split ▶ *See* Reverse Stock Split.

Negotiable An item that can be traded or transferred freely. Also refers to any part of a transaction where, for instance, a fee or, commission or interest rate can be negotiable, i.e. agreed to the satisfaction of one or more parties.

Net Any figure from which some liability, such as tax, has been deducted.

Net Asset Value Valuation of a company, or fund, based on its assets. This can lead to differences of perception depending on how assets are valued. For mutual funds and unit trusts this is calculated daily by dividing the net value by the number of outstanding shares. This is the price at which investors can redeem their mutual fund shares.
> *See also* Mutual Fund.

Net Cash Flow Retained earnings plus depreciation.
> *See also* Retained Earnings.

Net Earnings The company's profit, which remains once all coupons on outstanding bonds, all taxes and all dividends on outstanding preferred shares have been settled.

Net Position Difference between long and short positions held by a dealer in a given market.

Net Present Value ▶ *See* Present Value.

Net Profit Trading profits after deducting the charges detailed in the profit and loss account such as tax, depreciation, auditors and directors fees.

Net Transaction A transaction whereby the investor is not charged a commission. If a company sells new issues, the underwriter's commission is incorporated in the issue price. A commission will only be charged in secondary market trading.

Net Worth A measure of the difference between the total value of assets and possessions and total indebtedness.

Netback Refers to the value of a crude oil once it has been refined and the products from it have been sold, taking into account freight and refining costs. Thus crude traded in a netback deal is sold at a price that reflects the value of the products it yields.

Netting A system whereby outstanding financial contracts can be settled at a net figure, i.e. receivables are offset against payables to reduce the credit exposure to a counterparty and to minimize settlement risk.

Neutral A market that displays neither bullish or bearish tendencies.
> *See also* Bear *and* Bull.

New Economy A reference to the fast-growing technology-oriented industries with global reach, mainly selling computers and software and involved in the Internet, electronic commerce and telecommunications. A key example of the shift to the 'new economy' was the listing of high-tech giants Microsoft and Intel in the blue-chip Dow Jones 30 industrial index in October 1999, replacing venerable labour-intensive 'old economy' institutions like tyre-maker Goodyear and retailer Sears.

New Issue A security that is being offered for sale in the primary market.
> *See also* IPO *and* Primary Market.

New York Mercantile Exchange ▷ *See* NYMEX.

New York Stock Exchange ▷ *See* NYSE

NIF Note issuance facility. Allows borrowers to offer short-term paper, usually three or six months, in their own names. Fund availability is guaranteed to the borrower by underwriting banks who buy any unsold notes at successive rollover dates or who provide a standby credit.

Nikkei 225 The Nikkei 225 index is the benchmark index for equity prices on the TSE. Like the Dow Jones it is a simple arithmetic average of the 225 largest stocks on the first section of the TSE. Futures on the Nikkei are traded in Osaka, Singapore and Chicago.

▧ **www.nni.nikkei.co.jp/** ▧

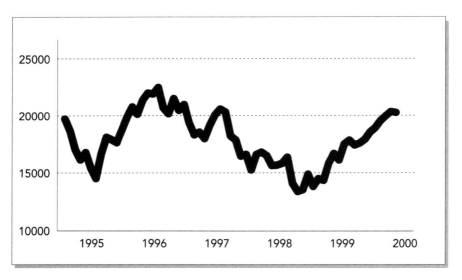

FIGURE 19 Nikkei 225

Nil Paid Rights Rights issues are typically offered at a discount to the prevailing market price of the existing securities, so the allotment letters have a market value and may be traded as 'nil paid rights' before payment for the new shares is due.

N/O A normal order to buy or sell at a certain level, i.e. to sell at higher or to buy at lower levels than prevailing market rates.

No-load Indicates that no mutual fund commission is charged.

No Par Value Shares with no par value assigned at the time the stock is authorized.

Nominal Interest Rates The interest rate expressed in money terms.

▷ *See also* Real Interest Rates.

Nominal Value ► *See* Face Value.

Nominee Account Securities that are owned by an investor but are registered in the name of the brokerage firm. The certificate bears the name of, and is held in safekeeping by, the brokerage firm. Records of the issuing company show the brokerage firm as the holder of the record. The brokerage firm records the investor as the beneficial owner. Also known as street name.

Non-competitive Bid Auction Bidding that does not include a yield, only the quantity. The investor then pays the average price determined by the competitive bidders. These bids allow small investors to participate in the auction. Since non-competitive bids are given priority and are awarded the full allocation, they could reduce the amounts available to competitive bidders.

Non-negotiable A transaction where the terms of the contract are fixed. Also, an instrument that can only be held by the original holder. It cannot be traded or transferred or used as collateral.

Non-performing Loan A loan on which neither interest payment nor principal repayment is being made. When a bank has such a loan on its books, it can either write it off against profits immediately or make loan loss provisions ready to make such a write-off in the future.

Non-voting Stock Securities that do not allow the holder to vote on company resolutions.

Normal Market Size The number of stocks that can be purchased without moving the market price.

North American Free Trade Agreement ► *See* NAFTA.

Note Issuance Facility ► *See* NIF.

Notional Bonds A standardized bond with hypothetical terms (coupon and maturity), which represents the basis for a bond futures contract.

Notional Principal The hypothetical amount on which interest payments are based in products such as interest rate swaps, FRAs, caps and floors.
► *See also* Cap, FRA, Floor *and* Swap.

NPV ► *See* Present Value.

NV Dutch company title: abbreviation of Naamloze Vennootschap.

NYMEX The New York Mercantile Exchange, which trades futures and options on precious metals and crude oil. ■ **www.nymex.com** ■

NYSE The New York Stock Exchange. ■ **www.nyse.com** ■

OAPEC Organization of Arab Petroleum Exporting Countries. Aims to improve economic co-operation in the petroleum industry. Members are Algeria, Bahrain, Egypt, Iraq, Kuwait, Libya, Qatar, Saudi Arabia, Syria and the United Arab Emirates.

OAT Obligations Assimilables du Trésor. Fungible Treasury bonds issued in France with maturities ranging from 7 to 30 years at fixed or floating interest.

OCO One cancels the other. A limit order that consists of two buy orders (or two sell orders) at different levels either side of the current market level. Execution of one order automatically cancels the other.

Odd Coupon This occurs when the first or last coupon period is longer or shorter than the normal coupon period.

Odd Date ▶ *See* Broken Date.

Odd Lot Trade A block of securities or commodities that is smaller or larger than the standard lot size traded in that market. The price can vary from the current market value.

ODR Ordinary Drawing Rights. Ordinary drawing rights. Similar to special drawing rights (SDRs). Also allocated to members of the IMF. However, ODRs are credits as opposed to SDRs, which are used as currency reserves in addition to a member nation's existing gold and dollar reserves.
   ▶ *See also* SDR.

OECD Organization for Economic Co-operation and Development. The OECD was set up to encourage financial stability and economic growth in its member countries. It also works with non-member countries and less developed nations. ▨ **www.oecd.org** ▨

Off Balance Sheet An obligation entered into by a company that does not have to show on the balance sheet. Examples are leases and project finance. With banks, where money earned is fee-based, examples include trading of swaps, options and letters of credit.
   ▶ *See also* Letter of Credit, Option *and* Swap.

Off-The-Run Issue Benchmark issues that are no longer the most recently issued in that maturity which tend to trade with a wider spread than the on-the-run issues.
   ▶ *See also* On-The-Run Issue.

Offer ▸ *See* Ask.

Offer Document Official document from a bidder in a takeover battle and which is sent to shareholders in the target company. In the US, can be synonymous with prospectus.
  ▸ *See also* Prospectus.

Offer for Sale/Subscription There are two main ways to bring new securities to listing. An offer for sale is a public invitation by a sponsoring intermediary to purchase new or existing securities. An offer for subscription or 'direct offer' is a direct invitation to the public by the issuer to subscribe for new securities.
  ▸ *See also* New Issue.

Offer Market A market in which there is more interest from sellers than buyers. Opposite of bid market.
  ▸ *See also* Bid Market.

Offshore Fund Funds based outside the tax system of the country in which prospective investors reside.

Oils Key products in international commodity and agricultural trade. The major oils are palm and soy.

Oligopoly Situation where a few firms selling an item control its supply and hence influence its price.

OM Stockholm The Swedish futures and options market which trades options on Swedish stocks as well as index and interest rate derivatives.
  ▪ **www.aso.se** ▪

Omega The currency risk involved in an options deal when the option writer or holder accounts for the transaction in a different currency.
  ▸ *See also* Option.

O/N Abbreviation for overnight. Used in swap and deposit transactions when the first value date is today and maturity falls tomorrow. The overnight swap price is adjusted by the interest rate differential for that short period.

O/N Funds Funds traded overnight on the interbank market to satisfy commercial banks' reserve requirements at the central bank.

O/N Limit Limits authorizing dealers to carry positions overnight. They are, therefore, not obliged to square the position at the end of the day.

On-The-Run Issue The most recent issue of a security, which would be trading with a narrower spread than the older, off-the-run, issues. As an issue ages its liquidity decreases and the spread tends to widen.

On Balance Volume A technical analysis indicator which assigns a value to the volume of contracts traded in each session. Buy or sell signals are indicated when a divergence between the on-balance volume and price is followed by a trend break in the on-balance volume.
  ▸ *See also* Technical Analysis.

OPEC Organization of Petroleum Exporting Countries, an association of the world's leading oil producing and exporting nations. OPEC's production quotas have a major bearing on oil prices.

OPEC's members are Algeria, Indonesia, Iran, Iraq, Kuwait, Libya, Nigeria, Qatar, Saudi Arabia, the United Arab Emirates and Venezuela.

▓ **www.opec.org** ▓

Open-end Management Company The legal name for a mutual fund.

▶ *See also* Investment Fund *and* Mutual Fund.

Open Interest A figure for the number of outstanding contracts on a futures contract which are not offset by an opposing futures transaction or fulfilled by delivery. In most cases, the open interest is measured on a daily basis. Reflects the degree of liquidity in that contract.

▶ *See also* Futures.

Open Market Operations Routine interventions by central banks in financial markets, usually the central bank sale or purchase of securities in the domestic money market intended to influence the volume of money and credit in the economy. Chiefly involves short-term government securities. Purchases inject reserves into the system to expand credit, while sales have the opposite effect.

▶ *See also* Fed.

Open Outcry An open-outcry market is one where buyers and sellers are brought together on a trading floor and cry out bids and offers to each other.

Open Position A position that has not yet been offset or closed.

Operating Margin The ratio of operating profit to turnover over a given period, expressed as a percentage and used to indicate a company's ability to control its variable costs.

Operating Profit After-tax earnings from a company's ordinary revenue-producing activities. Exact definitions vary from country to country.

Operational Balances Commercial bank funds held on deposit at the central bank to settle the final position at the end of the day between the banking system and the central bank.

Option An option gives the buyer or holder the right, but not the obligation, to buy or sell an underlying financial asset or commodity. Unlike futures, where the buyer has to fulfil the contract, an option gives the choice of whether to exercise or not. An option contract specifies a future date on or before which it can be exercised. This date is known as the expiry date. The price of an option – the 'strike' or 'exercise' price – is the price at which it can be exercised.

Options are very flexible instruments: they allow investors to benefit from favourable price movements while limiting the consequence of unfavourable price movements. Options holders have to pay a 'premium' for this protection as with any insurance contract.

There are two kinds of option. A call, which gives the holder the right to buy the underlying, and a put, which gives the holder the right to sell the underlying. More than one option transaction can be combined to create a spread. These strategies usually involve the simultaneous purchase and sale of options with different prices, or expiry dates, within the same class.

Options can be traded on a recognized exchange or over the counter (OTC).

▶ *See also* Derivatives, Futures *and* Spread.

Option Holder An individual who pays a premium for the right to buy or sell the underlying under an option contract.

Option Premium The price paid for an option. The premium, comprising intrinsic value plus time value, is paid by the holder to the writer for value spot.

Option Series Option contracts on the same underlying all having the same expiry date and strike price.

Option Strategies Combinations of calls and puts to create strategies for hedging and speculation. Examples are bull spread, bear spread, butterfly spread, condor spread, risk reversal, straddle and strangle.

Option Writer An institution that sells an option and thereby commits to buy or sell the underlying at a predetermined strike price in exchange for the premium paid by the option holder.

Optional Dividend A dividend that is payable either in cash or stock form. The shareholder is allowed to choose which method of payment to take.

Order Driven A market is described as being order driven when investors submit, buy and sell orders to a central location where they are then matched. Such markets are continuous auction markets. An example of an order-driven market is the NYSE.

▶ *See also* NYSE *and* Quote Driven.

Ordinary Capital Capital in a company that is entitled to the residue of profits and assets after senior debt and creditors have been satisfied.

Ordinary Drawing Rights ▶ *See* ODR.

Ordinary Share Capital Ordinary shares represent ownership in a limited liability company. Shareholders are entitled to dividends when they are declared by the company board of directors. Shareholders also have the last claim on the assets and income. They appoint and approve the company directors and usually have one vote for each share they hold.

Ordinary shares are the most widely traded of all securities due to continued liquidity and more the ease of ownership transfer from one investor to another.

Ordinary shares are known as common stock in the US.

▶ *See also* Preference Share.

Organization of Arab Petroleum Exporting Countries ▶ *See* OAPEC.

Organization for Economic Co-operation and Development ▶ *See* OECD.

Organization of Petroleum Exporting Countries ▶ *See* OPEC.

Oscillator Used in technical analysis, the oscillator is an indicator which moves back and forth between an upper and lower boundary. The oscillator attempts to indicate buy and sell signals by graphing the difference between a short- and long-term simple moving average. Oscillators are generally used only in ranging markets.
▶ *See also* Moving Average *and* Technical Analysis.

OSE Osaka Securities Exchange. ▮ **www.ose.or.jp** ▮

OTC Over the counter. A market conducted directly between dealers and principals via a telephone and computer network rather than via an exchange trading floor.

Out of the Money An option is described as being out of the money when the current price of the underlying is below the strike or exercise price for a call, and above the strike price for a put.
Options can also be described as being deep out of the money when they are likely to expire out of the money.
▶ *See also* In the Money, At the Money *and* Option.

Outright Purchases Government securities purchased outright by the authorities, i.e. with no agreement to subsequently sell them through a repurchase pact or reverse repo.

Overbought When prices have risen more than they should according to fundamental factors. This could mean the market is liable to a downward correction.
In technical analysis, an instrument is overbought when it registers more than 75 per cent on its RSI. Opposite of oversold.
▶ *See also* Oversold, RSI *and* Technical Analysis.

Overnight ▶ *See* O/N.

Oversold When prices have dropped more than they should according to fundamental factors. This could mean the market is liable to an upward correction.
In technical analysis, an instrument is oversold when it registers less than 25 per cent on its RSI.
▶ *See also* Overbought, RSI *and* Technical Analysis.

Oversubscribed When an issuing house receives more subscriptions for a new issue than are available. The issue will then be allocated, typically on a pro rata basis, and the issue will tend to open at a premium to represent the over-demand.

Overvalued A term implying that a security or currency is trading at a price higher than it should be relative to fundamental factors. Opposite of undervalued.
▶ *See also* Undervalued.

Oy Finnish company title: abbreviation of Osakeyhito.

Pac Man Defence Tactics used in the US to avoid a takeover, whereby the potential victim attempts to take over the predator. Named after a popular video game.

Paid Up Capital Shares for which the company has received full nominal value in payment. Callable capital is that part of a share for which the company has not received payment.

Panamax A vessel that can move through the Panama Canal. Usually means a vessel below 65,000 long dwt.

Paper Colloquially, refers to any securities.

Paper Barrel A cargo of oil traded for short-term hedging or speculative purposes but not usually physically delivered.
> *See also* Hedging.

Paper Chain ▷ *See* Daisy Chain.

Paper Profit Apparent, and as yet unrealized, profit arising out of an increase in the value of an asset.

Par Bond Bond issued at par or, in debt restructurings, swapped for old debt at par to provide debt service reduction.

Par Value ▷ *See* Face Value.

Parallel Loans ▷ *See* Back-to-back Loans.

Pari Passu Securities issued with a pari passu clause rank equally with existing securities of the same class.

Paris Club An *ad hoc* forum for Western creditor governments to discuss the renegotiation of debt owed to official creditors or guaranteed by them.
> *See also* London Club.

Parity Equality. Used in FX markets to describe when a currency rate matches its official benchmark value. In the ERM an exchange rate is at parity when it equals its central rate.
> *See also* ERM *and* FX.

Participation Part ownership by a company or government in an oil venture or operation. Also refers to a mortgage loan made jointly by two or more lenders.

Participation Certificate In the US, represents an interest in mortgage loans. The buyer receives the cash flows and is the owner financially, although the seller remains the mortgagee of record.

In Switzerland, a non-voting form of equity issued by Swiss companies.

Partly Paid A system of payment that allows shareholders or bondholders to pay only part of the determined price for a new issue, the rest being settled on a fixed future date.

Passive Management An investment strategy that focuses on mirroring the composition of a given market or sector to match its return and risk characteristics.

▶ *See also* Active Fund Management.

Pass-through Certificate Represents an interest in a pool of mortgages on which payments received on the underlying pool are passed through to the investor by the firm servicing the mortgage payments.

Passing the Dividend A dividend is passed, i.e. not paid, for various reasons, sometimes lack of funds, but also when a company is in a recovery phase.

Patterns The formations of various shapes that prices on a chart create. Patterns are used by technical analysts to identify reversals, continuation of trends and the strength of trends.

▶ *See also* Technical Analysis.

Pay Date The date when a dividend is due to a shareholder.

Paydown Amount by which, in a US Treasury refunding, the par value of maturing securities is greater than that of those being sold.

Payer of Fixed In the interest rate swap market, refers to the fixed side of the contract. A payer of fixed is one who pays the fixed amount and receives floating. Opposite of receiver of fixed.

Paying Agent Institution appointed to supervise payment and, for floating rate notes, sets bond issues rates.

Payment Date The date on which a coupon payment, dividend payments or fund distribution is due to be made.

Payout Ratio Portion of net profits paid in dividends.

Payrolls Nickname used in financial markets to refer to US non-farm payrolls – a key barometer of the state of the economy. More generally used to describe an employer's financial record of employees' salaries.

PDF Portable Document Format. A file format developed by Adobe to transmit documents in their original format.

P/E Ratio (PER) The price earnings ratio. Calculated by dividing the share price by a company's EPS. This ratio is one of the most important ratios to determine investment value and is widely used by the media as an indicator of whether a stock is expensive or cheap. It states how many years of earnings have been priced into the stock. The higher the PER, the higher the market values of the company's earnings.

▶ *See also* EPS *and* PEG Ratio.

P/E RATIO (PRICE/EARNINGS RATIO, PER)

The net profit for the latest reported 12-month period divided by the latest closing share price. If a company has an EPS of 10 and a share price of 150, its P/E is 15. In other words, it would take fifteen years for the stock investment to pay for itself. The reverse of the P/E ratio is the 'earnings yield', or 1/PER. A company with a P/E of 15 has an earnings yield of 6.66 percent (1 divided by 15).

Average P/E ratios for stock market indices historically range between 10 and 20, but for some individual companies the ratio might swing wildly, from less than three to 1,000 or more, depending on investors' outlook for the share. Sometimes even stock market indices have average P/Es of 50 or more, as was the case in Japan in the late 1980s and the US NASDAQ market at the start of this century.

To calculate a forecast (or 'prospective') P/E, analysts make a forecast for EPS and then divide today's share price by the forecast EPS.

If investors expect a company's earnings to triple every year in the next five years, they will have no problem paying a historical (or 'trailing') P/E of 1,000, because the P/E for Forecast Year 1 would be 333; for FY 2 the P/E would fall to 111; and so on. A relatively low P/E means investors' outlook for the company is gloomy, and that they do not want to buy the share even at that low multiple.

P/E ratios cannot be considered in isolation, but must be compared against industry and national averages. Low-growth companies such as steel makers, shipyards and construction companies often trade at relatively low P/Es (10 or less) while high-tech firms often command P/E multiples of 40 or more.

The P/E ratio is the most widely used measure of corporate valuation, because it is easy to understand and widely available in financial newspapers. But it also has many flaws. The divider – net profit – is subject to the vagaries of accounting standards, depreciation regimes, interest rate levels and corporate tax rates. Two companies having the same cash flow may have very different bottom-line net profits. That is why analysts increasingly use price/EBITDA (earnings before interest, taxation, depreciation and amortization).

If a company has no earnings, which is often the case with high-tech start-ups, investors will look higher up on the profit and loss account

▶

and relate the stock price to sales in order to work out the price/sales ratio (stock price divided by sales per share).

The divider of the P/E ratio – market capitalization – is not a perfect measure of the total cost of the company either. Two companies with a market capitalization of $1 billion and net profit would each have a P/E of 10. But if company A has debt of one billion, while company is debt-free, the P/E ratio would not highlight this. Therefore, analysts replace market cap by 'enterprise value', which is the sum of market cap, plus debt, minus cash and gives a much better perspective on the true value of a listed company.

So far, the ultimate sophistication of the P/E ratio is the enterprise value/EBITDA ratio, which measures both value and risk and eliminates the distortion of national depreciation rates, interest rates and tax regimes. Its drawback is that it requires a lot of homework.

Formula: Share Price/EPS.

Example (based on Reuters share price of 12.92 GBP at the close on Friday 7 April, 2000):
Reuters 1999 P/E = 12.92/0.302 = 42.78
Reuters 2000 P/E = 12.92/0.276 = 46.81
Reuters 2001 P/E = 12.92/0.306 = 42.22
Comparative trailing P/Es for Reuters, its main country index and its sector index:

Reuters P/E:	42.78
FTSE All share index P/E:	26.70
FTSE Media & Photography index P/E: 73.90	

Peaks/Troughs Terms used by technical analysts. Peaks, or reaction highs, are resistance points and represent a price level where selling pressure overcomes buying pressure, causing the price advance to reverse. Troughs, or reaction lows, are support points and represent a price level where buying pressure overcomes selling pressure, leading the price fall to turn back.
▶ *See also* Technical Analysis.

PEG Ratio Price earning growth ratio. Calculated by dividing a stock's prospective P/E ratio by a share of the estimated future growth rate in EPS. The PEG ratio was invented by 1960s market guru, Jim Slater, who used it as his main investing criteria. Consensus estimates are used to derive the P/E ratio and EPS used in the calculation.
▶ *See also* Consensus Estimates.

Pennants ▶ *See* Flags/Pennants.

Penny Stocks A type of ordinary share, which is of negligible value but which may prove to be a good speculative investment. In the US, a share priced at less than one dollar and in the UK at less than one pound.
▶ *See also* Ordinary Share.

PER ▶ *See* P/E Ratio.

Performing Loan A loan is performing if the borrower is paying the interest on it.
▶ *See also* Non-performing Loan.

Perpetual Note A floating-rate note that has no final maturity. For this privilege, the borrower pays a higher margin over a relevant base interest rate. As they will never be repaid, the notes assume the characteristics of an equity issue.

Petro Dollars A term prevalent in the 1970s to describe the abundance of dollars held and invested by the OPEC nations when it pushed up oil prices.

Pfandbriefe German bonds issued to refinance mortgages or public projects. Can only be issued by specially authorized banks, which are also fully liable for each issue. They are secured by mortgage or public sector loans.
Pfandbriefe are officially quoted on German stock exchanges, while issuers maintain a secondary market.

PHLX Philadelphia Stock Exchange. A US stock market that also lists currency derivatives. ■ **www.phlx.com** ■

Physical market ▶ *See* Spot Market.

PIBOR Paris Interbank Offered Rate. The rate at which banks are prepared to lend money market funds to each other.

Pip Price movements are expressed in terms of pips or points. Pip is usually synonymous with point, although may refer to one-tenth of a point.
▶ *See also* Point.

Pit A section, often self-contained, on an exchange floor for the trading of a particular type of financial instrument or commodity.
▶ *See also* Open Outcry.

Placing A 'private' method of selling a new stock issue usually directly to institutional investors, bypassing the public.
▶ *See also* Flotation *and* IPO.

Plain Vanilla Standard financial or derivative instruments without special features.
▶ *See also* Exotic.

Planned Economy An economy where the government fixes prices and production.

Platinum Share Similar to a golden share. One version is for use if an administrator, receiver or liquidator is likely to be appointed to a parent company. The platinum share could be used to safeguard a relatively stable subsidiary.

Platt's An international oil price reporting agency which specializes in data and news for the oil markets. A unit of Standard & Poor's Information Group.
■ **www.platts.com** ■

Plaza Agreement An agreement among the Group of Five Nations in 1985 to promote further depreciation of the US dollar.

Plc A UK company title: abbreviation of public limited company.

Ploughed Back Earnings that are reinvested in the company and not distributed.

PMI Purchasing manager's index. These indices, now produced in a number of countries, are leading indicators of economic activity, based on a monthly survey of purchasing managers.
▶ *See also* Economic Indicators.

Point Price movements are expressed in terms of points.
▶ *See also* Pip.

Point and Figure Chart A price chart that captures pure price movement with no regard for time or volume. Rising prices are denoted by a column of Xs and falling prices by a column of Os. Subsequent columns are placed to the right of earlier columns.
Point and figure charts are not widely used because they have to be hand drawn.
▶ *See also* Technical Analysis.

Poison Pill Actions taken by a company to outwit a predator in a potential hostile takeover. Examples are the issue of high yielding bonds, conditional rights to

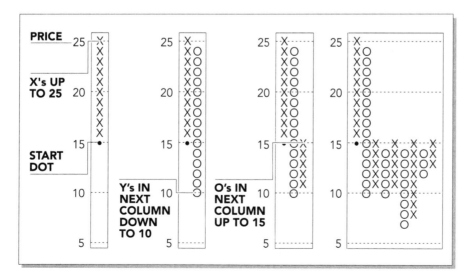

FIGURE 20 Point and Figure Chart

shareholders to buy shares at a large discount if the takeover succeeds or making massive long-term commitments to the company's pension funds.

Political Risk The risk associated with investing in politically unstable countries.

POP Public Offering Price. The new issue price fixed by the underwriter on behalf of a company. The underwriter's commission is built into the price. Shares in a mutual fund may be purchased at the POP.

Portable Document Format ▶ *See* PDF.

Portal Short for web portal, a portal is a website that offers features beyond information such as search engines and e-commerce facilities.

Portfolio An investor's collection, or holding, of financial instruments.

Portfolio Manager Designated advisor who manages a portfolio of investments on behalf of an investor, often with full authority to take decisions. Known as acting on a discretionary basis.

Position Balance of purchases and sales in a given financial instrument for a given maturity.
▶ *See also* Short, Long *and* Flat.

Position Keeping The monitoring of a dealer's position.

Position Limit Maximum position, either net long or short, which may be held by a dealer, a group of dealers or a dealing room.

Positive Carry Where the financing cost of a position is less than the return.

PPP Purchasing Power Parity. A means of comparing living standards between various nations. PPP aims to cut out translation distortions, such as translating the gross domestic product into one basic currency.

Praecipuum Part of a management fee assessed on the full principal amount of a new issue to compensate the lead manager for taking responsibility for handling the issue.

Pre-Emptive Rights ▶ *See* Rights.

Pre-Market Trading Takes place before the official opening of business on the trading floor of an exchange.

Pre-Marketing Meeting of investment bankers with potential investors before an IPO or second offering to determine potential demand.

Precious Metals There are eight precious or noble metals – gold, silver, platinum, palladium, rhodium, iridium, osmium and ruthenium. The latter four are co-products of platinum and palladium.

Preferential Issue A certain percentage of a share offer to the public, which is set aside for subscriptions from employees.

Preference Share Preference or preferred shares entitle a holder to a prior claim on any dividend paid by the company on ordinary shares, or to its assets in the event of a liquidation. Typically these shares do not carry voting or pre-emptive rights.

▶ *See also* Ordinary Share.

Premium Generally used to describe when something is trading above its normal price. An asset or fund is described as being at premium when its market price is above its face value. In the capital markets it is the amount by which a bond sells above par. In foreign exchange terms it is the margin by which the forward rate is higher than the spot. Opposite of discount.

▶ *See also* Discount.

Prepayment In mortgages, any unscheduled principal payment made in addition to the normal amortization.

Present Value The current value of a future cash flows, discounted at an appropriate interest rate.

Presold Term used when a new security issue has been sold out before all issue details have been announced. In bond issues, this would indicate that sufficient orders for the issue were placed before the final terms announcement.

Price Channel Used in technical analysis. Provides buy and sell signals by indicating when a value moves outside set deviation limits. The channel chart consists of two bands either side of a simple moving average. Channels can also be used on volume charts and as an overbought/oversold indicator.

▶ *See also* Moving Average *and* Technical Analysis.

Price Driven Trading where prices set by the market makers determine the order flow. Also known as quote driven.

▶ *See also* Order Driven.

Price Earnings Ratio ▶ *See* P/E Ratio.

Price Earnings Growth Ratio ▶ *See* PEG Ratio.

Price Indicators Measure both the levels and rates of change in groups of prices from the price of a basket of goods purchased by the average consumer to the prices paid at the factory gate.

▶ *See also* Economic Indicators.

Price Volume Index A technical analysis indicator. Essentially a volume-weighted RSI, which attempts to measure the strength of money entering and leaving the market.

▶ *See also* Moving Average, RSI *and* Technical Analysis.

Primary Commodities Commodities in a raw or unprocessed state, e.g. iron ore.

Primary Dealer Dealers who are authorized by the central bank to deal in the primary market for government securities. Primary dealers in the government bond markets are normally required to make significant contributions to auctions; act as market makers in the secondary market and keep the central bank well informed of market conditions and developments.

Primary dealers can also be known as primary distributors, jobbers, SVTs (France), underwriters and lead managers.

▶ *See also* Primary Markets.

Primary Markets Primary markets are markets where new issues of securities take place. Any subsequent resale or purchase of such securities is handled on the secondary market.

▶ *See also* Secondary Market.

Primary Offer ▶ *See* IPO.

Prime Bank A prime bank is one of the highest rank.

Prime Rate The borrowing rate charged by banks to their best customers.

Principal The total amount borrowed or invested, e.g. the face amount of a bond bought by an investor.

Print Money A term used to describe when a government increases the money supply. This can be achieved in a number of ways including actually printing more bank notes or issuing new debt which is bought by the central bank.

Prior Charges Charges on senior debt such as debentures, loan stock and notes that rank ahead of ordinary share capital.

Private Placement Usually refers to a bond issue placed directly with investors, not listed on a stock exchange, and without a prospectus.

▶ *See also* Placing.

Privatization The act of governments selling their state-owned commercial and industrial concerns to the private sector.

Pro Rata Sinking Fund A sinking fund where each investor gives up an equal percentage of holdings to the issuer when the issue is called for sinking fund retirements. Typically only applied to registered securities.

▶ *See also* Purchase Fund *and* Sinking Fund.

Profit and Loss Account A summary of all the expenditure and income of a company over a set period of time. Also called an income statement.

Profit Margin Net profit as a percentage of sales or capital.

Profit-taking Realizing profits by closing out an existing position.

Programme-trading Computer-based trading technique, used in markets, based on the flow of trading and price levels rather than fundamental data. Usually aims to exploit arbitrage possibilities between stock index futures/options and underlying equities.

Promissory Note A note representing a promise by the issuer to repay a loan. Promissory notes are not classed as securities. Failure to pay a promissory note renders the borrower immediately liable to be sued for payment.

Prompt Date The date on which a commodity must be delivered to fulfil a contract.

Prospectus Document provided by the issuing company giving detailed terms and conditions of a new stock or debt offering.

Protectionism Imposition of customs duties on imports so as to protect a domestic industry from cheaper competitive products. It can involve import restrictions, export subsidies and non-tariff moves such as health and environment regulations.

Protocol An agreed format for transmitting data between two or more devices.

Provisions Long-term liability that appears on a balance sheet, such as an employee pension scheme.
> *See also* Assets/Liabilities.

Proxy A written authorization by a shareholder for another party, or a company's board of directors, to cast votes at a shareholder meeting.

PSBR Public Sector Borrowing Requirement in the UK. The negative difference between the government's revenue and expenditure, which means it is still borrowing. When the difference is a positive value it is known as the PSDR – public sector debt repayment.

PSDR > *See* PSBR.

Pte Singapore company title: abbreviation of private.

Pty Australian company title: abbreviation of proprietary.

Public Offering Price > *See* POP.

Public Placement A public bond placement is offered generally to a market, usually listed on a stock exchange and in relatively small denominations. Usually costs the borrower more than a private placement.

Public Sector Borrowing Requirements > *See* PSBR.

Public Sector Debt Repayment > *See* PSBR.

Publicly Traded Fund > *See* Closed-end Fund.

Purchase Fund Similar to a sinking fund but not mandatory. The borrower will purchase bonds in the market if available at par or below.
> *See also* Pro Rata Sinking Fund.

Purchase Price A purchase price becomes legally enforceable on both buyer and seller once a written order to buy has been accepted by the vendor.

Purchasing Manager's Index > *See* PMI.

Purchasing Power Parity > *See* PPP.

Purgatory and Hell Bond A variation of a heaven and hell bond. It is a bond whose proceeds from redemption are tied to the maturity spot exchange rate of another currency against the bond's denominated currency.
> *See also* Heaven *and* Hell Bonds.

Put Call Parity The relationship between a put and a call European style, based on the same underlying, exercise price and expiry date.

▷ *See also* Option.

Put/Call Ratio The number of puts traded in relation to the number of calls traded in the market. This ratio is an indicator of market sentiment.

▷ *See also* Option.

Put An option giving the buyer or the holder the right to sell the underlying at an agreed price within a specified time. The seller or writer has the obligation to buy.

▷ *See also* Call.

Put Through ▷ *See* Cross.

Puttable A bond is described as puttable or having a put feature when the holder has the right to sell the bond back to the issuer at a specific date before maturity. The repurchase price, which may be at par, premium or discount, is specified at the time of issue.

▷ *See also* Callable.

Qualified Accounts The published balance sheet and accounts of a company, in which the auditors' report expresses any reservations as to whether a true and fair view of the company's activities has been presented.

Quantitative Analysis Quantitative analysis involves the statistical study of historic returns, price volatility and price correlations of different assets to construct optimal portfolios. It relies heavily on mathematical models such as CAPM and DDM.
> ▶ *See also* CAPM, Fundamental Analysis *and* Technical Analysis.

Quick Ratio Sometimes called the acid test. Indicator of a company's ability to meet its short-term liabilities. Within industries, higher quick ratios suggest relatively high liquidity. It is calculated like a current ratio in that it measures a company's current assets relative to its liabilities. However, stock or inventory is excluded from the assets because it cannot be sold quickly.
> ▶ *See also* Current Ratio.

QUICK RATIO

Current assets minus inventory, divided by current liabilities. The quick ratio is more stringent than the current ratio: it excludes inventories from current assets because inventories cannot always be readily converted into cash. That is why it is also known as the 'acid test'.

Its normal range is between 0.5 and 1.5, with a value of 1.0 being considered very solid. It means a company could pay off all its short-term liabilities from its cash balances plus its accounts receivable. For most companies, such a high level of liquidity is not deemed necessary.

For large, listed companies with easy access to the capital markets, the current and quick ratios are less relevant for the investor, since these companies can always find short-term finance to meet short-term obligations. But a company receiving a large order from a small, private company will want to check its client's financial solidity. That is when current and quick ratios become all-important.

Formula: (Current Assets – Inventory)/Current Liabilities.
or: (Cash + Receivables)/ Current Liabilities.

Example
Data from Reuters' 1999 annual report (in million GBP):
Reuters quick ratio = (1,447 – 4)/1,679 = 0.85.
Since Reuters has very little inventory (it sells services, not goods), its current and quick ratio are virtually the same.

Quotation Current price or rate given in the market or exchange, but not necessarily the price at which a trade will be made.

Quote Driven A market is described as being quote driven when registered market makers are required to display bid and offer prices, and in some cases the maximum bargain size to which these prices relate. The London SEAQ system and NASDAQ are examples of quote driven markets.
▶ *See also* NASDAQ, Order Driven *and* SEAQ.

Quoted Currency The currency quoted against the base currency, i.e. the numerator quoted in terms of the denominator. For example, the quoted currency in the US dollar/euro quotation is the euro.
▶ *See also* Base Currency.

R&D Research and development.

Rally General trading term for when a whole market or a sector reverses a previous general fall or is a move up from a narrow trading range.

Range Forward ▶ *See* Risk Reversal.

Ranking Denotes where a bond stands in relation to priority claims from a lender upon default by the borrower. Senior debt earns high priority if lenders have to reclaim funds, hence the bond issue terms can be less onerous for the borrower. Subordinated debt ranks a bond lower down the scale, thus a borrower has to offer a lender more advantageous terms.

RAN Revenue anticipation notes.
▶ *See also* Municipal Notes.

Rate of Change ▶ *See* ROC.

Rate of Return The return on an investment. For a company this would be net profits expressed as a percentage of average capital employed.

Ratio Analysis Determination of the prospective future performance of a company. An analysis of a company's accounts involving examining three kinds of ratios – profitability, liquidity and balance sheet ratios.

Real Interest Rates The actual rate of return calculated by deducting the inflation rate from the current interest rate. Also known as real yield.
▶ *See also* Nominal Interest Rates.

Real-time Data Term used to describe live prices as opposed to historical data.

Real Yield ▶ *See* Real Interest Rates.

Realized Gain The cash profit from liquidating of a position.

Realized Loss The cash loss from liquidating of a position.

Receivables Outstanding debts due to a company.

Receiver A receiver is appointed by creditors to take control of a bankrupt or insolvent company's assets.
▶ *See also* Bankruptcy *and* Insolvency.

Recession A period of static or negative economic growth. Various nations have differing definitions but the US definition of two succeeding quarters of negative growth is widely used.

Record Date The date on which a shareholder must be the official owner of shares to be entitled to the dividend. This date is set by the board of directors.
  ▶ *See also* Ex *and* Ex-Dividend.

Rectangle A technical analysis pattern that represents a pause in a trend in which prices move sideways between two parallel trendlines. A rectangle portrays a consolidation period in the main trend and is generally resolved in the direction of that trend. Also known as a trading range or congestion area.
  ▶ *See* Technical Analysis.

Red Book An annual statement in the UK that accompanies the budget. It is published by the Government and contains detailed information on announced measures.

Red Herring US term for the preliminary prospectus for a new issue, which may be used to obtain an indication of the market's interest in that security. Key figures are left blank, such as issue price, profit and dividend forecast.
  Business is not conducted on the basis of a preliminary statement and in the US the law demands a red notice be printed to that effect on the face of the document, giving rise to the phrase 'red herring'.

Redemption The repurchase of a bond at maturity by the issuer.

Redemption Warrant The borrower offers the holder a guaranteed redemption price if the warrant is not exercised.
  ▶ *See also* Warrant.

Redemption Yield Current yield increased or decreased to take account of the capital gain or loss on redemption.

Rediscount Purchase before maturity by a central bank of a government obligation or other financial instrument already discounted in the money market.

Refinancing The issuing of new debt to replace old. A borrower pays off one loan with the proceeds from another provided by other lenders. If the lenders are effectively the same then it could technically be called a rescheduling. Bankers might use the term refinancing.
  ▶ *See also* Restructuring.

Refinery Plant used to separate the various components present in crude oil and convert them into end-user products or feedstock for other manufacturing processes.

Refining Processing a raw material into a pure state, in particular metals and sugar.

Refunding Rollover of government debt by replacing one issue with another, the maturity of which is deferred to a later date.

Refunding Operations The quarterly auction of US Treasury securities with maturities of three and ten years in the months of February, May, August and

November, together with the semi-annual auction of the 30-year in February and August all form part of the refunding operations of the US Treasury.

Registered Form A security that is registered in the books of the issuer in the name of the owner. Securities are kept in either registered or bearer form and government bonds are most commonly registered.
▶ *See also* Bearer Shares/Bearer Forms.

Registrar The body responsible for keeping a record of the company's shareholders. When securities are dealt in book entry form and no certificates are issued, it is particularly important to have an accurate list of shareholders.

Reinvestment Risk The risk that future cash flows from a particular investment will be reinvested at a lower rate of return.

Relative Performance Compares the performance of a security against an index.

Relative Strength Comparison between a current share price, portfolio of shares or a stock index and the price of the same instrument at a given time in the past.

Relative Strength Index ▶ *See* RSI.

Repo ▶ *See* Repurchase Agreement.

Repo Market ▶ *See* Gensaki Market.

Repo Rate A simple interest rate calculation to determine how much interest is to be added on to the second leg of a repo transaction.
▶ *See also* Repurchase Agreement.

Reporting Dealer In the US, primary dealers first have to achieve the status of reporting dealer, whereby they report their positions and trading volumes to the Federal Reserve.

Repurchase Agreement A repurchase agreement or repo is a transaction in which one party sells a security to another party while agreeing to repurchase it from the counterparty at some date in the future, at a pre-agreed price.
Repos allow traders to short-sell securities and allow the owners of securities to earn added income by lending the securities they own.
Through this operation the counterparty is effectively a borrower of funds to finance further purchases of securities and pays interest to the holder. The rate of interest used is known as the repo rate.
Reverse repo is the reverse situation, whereby the counterparty is a lender of funds.
Some central banks use repos as part of their money market operations.

Required Return The rate of return used by investors to decide whether an investment is attractive or not.

Rescheduling A borrower delays redemption of principal under the terms of a new repayment schedule. Interest continues to be paid and the rate of interest can be raised or lowered.
▶ *See also* Refinancing *and* Restructuring.

Reserve Currency Internationally accepted currency and is used by central banks to meet their financial commitments.

Reserve Requirements Percentage of deposits that, by law, depository institutions must set aside in their vaults or with their central bank. Lowering or raising this requirement influences the money supply. A reduction in reserve requirements enables banks to increase lending while an increase forces them to reduce lending. Sometimes known as minimum reserve requirements, registered reserves or reserve ratio.

Reserves A company's reserves are primarily profits retained in the business and accumulated over the years rather than paid out by way of dividends. They are usually held as cash or in highly liquid assets. Shareholders have no rights over reserves so that a company can disburse them or not, as it sees fit, within the usual accounting rules.

The term reserves is also used to describe the official foreign exchange reserves held by governments to ensure they can meet current and near term claims.

▶ *See also* Dividends *and* Retained Earnings.

Resistance Resistance is a level, usually identified on a price chart, where selling interest is strong enough to overcome buying pressure so that the price does not rise beyond the resistance level. Each time a level of resistance is penetrated it will create a new level of support.

▶ *See also* Support *and* Trendline.

Restructuring A process whereby a borrower arranges to replace debt of one maturity with debt of another maturity.

▶ *See also* Refinancing *and* Rescheduling.

Retail Price Index ▶ *See* RPI.

Retained Earnings Earnings not paid out as dividends by a company. Typically reinvested back into the business. Retained earnings are an important component of shareholders' equity.

▶ *See also* Reserves.

Retracement Percentage retracements are used by technical analysts to determine price objectives. Markets usually retrace previous moves by predictable percentages such as 33, 50 and 67. The 33 and 67 are Dow theory minimum and maximum retracements. The 50 retracement is the most important according to Gann. The Fibonacci number sequence refines these numbers to produce retracements of 61.8, 38 and 50 per cent.

▶ *See also* Dow Theory *and* Technical Analysis.

Return on Assets ▶ *See* ROA.

Return on Capital Employed ▶ *See* ROCE.

Return on Equity ▶ *See* ROE.

Revaluation Formal upward adjustment of a currency's official par value or central exchange rate. Opposite of devaluation.

▶ *See also* Devaluation.

Reversal In technical analysis, a reversal is a change in trend. Many technical analysts use patterns in price charts to spot a reversal. Key reversal patterns include head and shoulders, triple top/bottom, double top/bottom and V-formation/spikes.

▶ *See also* Patterns *and* Technical Analysis.

Reversal Day A term used in technical analysis. A key reversal day marks an important turning point on a chart but it cannot be correctly identified until prices have moved significantly in the opposite direction to the previous trend.

A top reversal day is defined as when a new high has been set in an uptrend and is followed by a lower close than the previous close. A bottom reversal day would be a new low followed by a close above the previous day's close.

An island reversal occurs when an upward gap has formed, prices have traded in a narrow range for a few days and a breakaway gap to the downside then occurs. This leaves the price action looking like an island, which indicates a trend reversal.

▶ *See also* Gap *and* Technical Analysis.

Reverse Cash and Carry Trade ▶ *See* Cash and Carry Trade.

Reverse Stock Split Reduction of the outstanding stocks of a company into a smaller number of stocks without cost to the shareholders who retain their proportionate holdings. This is not as common as a stock split and is usually only seen when the stock price is low. Also known as a negative stock split.

▶ *See also* Stock Split.

Reverse Takeover Where a company takes over a larger concern or when an unlisted company takes over a concern that is listed on a stock exchange.

Revolving Line of Credit A bank line of credit for which customers pay fees and can then take money according to their needs. Also known as a revolver.

Rich Cheap Analysis Rich and cheap refers to the pricing of a security relative to comparable securities in the secondary market. It is measured using standard deviation. A new issue is considered to be cheap if it is inexpensive compared to the rest of the market.

▶ *See also* Cheap *and* Standard Deviation.

Rights Issue One of the ways a company can raise additional funds, which must be offered to current shareholders first. A rights issue allows a shareholder to buy an additional number of shares for each share held, e.g. a two for three rights issue entitles shareholders to buy two additional shares for every three owned. Rights can be traded in the market.

Risk The probability that an investment or venture will make a loss or not make the returns expected. This probability can be measured.

There are many different types of risk including basis risk, country or sovereign risk, credit risk, currency risk, economic risk, inflation risk, liquidity risk, market or systematic risk, liquidity risk, political risk, settlement risk, systemic risk and translation risk.

Risk–Return Relationship The relationship between risk and return. To achieve greater returns an investor must take greater risks.

Risk Management Risk management is a 'middle office' function that sits between the dealing room and settlement. It involves revaluing all positions at least daily to estimate the risk of possible future losses on those positions, and ensure they are.
▶ *See also* Middle Office *and* Mark to Market.

Risk Reversal An option strategy involving the purchase of a put and the sale of a call, or vice versa, with different strike levels. The premium generated from the sale of an option could partly or totally finance the premium to be paid for the purchase of an option. Also known as a cylinder, a break forward or range forward.
▶ *See also* Option.

ROA Return on Assets. A company's ability to operate profitably can be measured directly by measuring its return on assets. This is done using three ratios, which are related but use different definitions of income and assets. Return on total assets (ROTA) is calculated as a ratio of the attributable profits for the last 12 months to total assets (fixed and current) for the same period,

ROA (RETURN ON ASSETS)

The ratio of a company's net profit to its total assets, expressed as a percentage.

ROA measures how well a company's management uses its assets to generate profits. It is a better measure of operating efficiency than ROE, which only measures how much profit is generated on the shareholders' equity, but ignores debt funding. This ratio is particularly relevant for banks, which typically have huge assets.

Some analysts use earnings before interest and taxes (EBIT) rather than net profit to measure operating efficiency, arguing that management has little influence on interest rate and taxation levels.

Formula: Net profit/Total Assets * 100.

Example

In 1999 Reuters had total assets of £2,652 million and net profits of £425 million.
Reuters' 1999 ROA: 425/2652 = 16.03 percent.

expressed as a percentage. It measures how effectively a company can generate earnings from its assets.

Return on fixed assets is the ratio of attributed profits to fixed assets alone, expressed as a percentage. It measures how effectively a company can generate earnings for its long-term assets such as land and machinery.

Return on net assets (RONA) – a popular ratio that measures attributable profits as a return to shareholders (shareholders' funds).

▶ *See also Assets, Earnings and Shareholders' Funds.*

ROC Rate of Change. In technical analysis, the ROC is an indicator that measures the ratio of the most recent closing price to a price in a previous set period. Thus, a five-day rate of change oscillator is constructed by dividing the latest closing price by the price five days previous and multiplying by 100. The 100 line becomes the midpoint or zero line.

▶ *See also* Oscillator *and* Technical Analysis.

ROCE Return on Capital Employed. The return on all the sources of finance used by shareholders. It is the ratio of operating profit to capital employed expressed as a percentage.

▶ *See also* Operating Profit.

ROCE (RETURN ON CAPITAL EMPLOYED)

ROCE is the ratio of operating profit (EBIT) to capital employed, expressed as a percentage. Capital employed equals shareholders' funds plus long-term liabilities – in other words, all the long-term funds used by the company. The ratio measures the return on all sources of finance used by the company (i.e. equity plus debt) and is very similar to return on assets (which includes current liabilities).

Formula: ROCE = EBIT/Total Capital Employed * 100.

Example

In 1999 Reuters earned an operating profit of £532 million. It had shareholders' equity of £601 million and long-term debt of £284 million. Reuters' 1999 ROCE = 532/(601 + 284 = 885) * 100 = 60.11 percent. Again, this ROCE is exceptionally high because Reuters reduced shareholders' equity in 1998. As shareholders' equity swells again in the coming years, ROCE should ease back to more normal levels.

ROE Return on Equity. The ratio of earnings to the total value of equity. Calculated using the earnings for shareholders (net income) for the most recently reported 12 months and the average value of equity over the same period.

ROE (RETURN ON EQUITY)

The ratio of a company's profit to its shareholders' equity, expressed as a percentage. It is the most widely used measure of how well management uses shareholders' funds.

Its main advantage is that it is a benchmark that allows investors to compare the profitability of hugely differing industries. Investors do not care whether their holdings are in low-margin retailers or high-margin technology companies, as long as they produce an above-average ROE.

Its main flaw is that it ignores the debt side of the company's funding and thus fails to measure the amount of risk involved in obtaining a given amount of earnings. A high ROE can be due to high earnings *or* low equity, therefore it is always wise to keep an eye on the company's leverage (as measured by its debt/equity ratio).

ROE ratios for healthy companies range between 10 and 25 per cent. Most investors look for companies with double-digit ROEs, or at least ROEs which are higher than the return on a risk-free investment such as a government bond. Companies earning high ROEs will typically attract competition into their market segment and need to keep growing and/or cutting costs to maintain double-digit ROE levels.

Formula: Attributable Profit/Shareholders' Equity * 100.

Example

In 1999, Reuters had net profits of £425 million and shareholders' equity of £601 million.
ROE = 425/601 * 100 = 70.71 per cent.
This exceptionally high ROE is due to the fact that in 1998 Reuters returned a large amount of cash to its shareholders, reducing shareholders' equity by £1,289 million that year. In the past decade and before the payout, Reuters' ROE ranged between 50 and 26 per cent.

Rolling Settlement   Settlement of securities on a recurring cycle of a certain number of days from the trade date, rather than on fixed account days.

Rollover   The periodic renewal of a loan, repriced at current market rates.

Rollover Date   The date on which FRNs pay their previous coupon and from when they start to accrue interest on their next coupon.
Will often be used as a flat, i.e. free of accrued interest, settlement date.
▶ *See also* FRN.

RONA   ▶ *See* Return on Assets.

ROTA   ▶ *See* Return on Assets.

Round Lot Trade The most common block of securities or commodities trading in that market.

Round Turn A transaction consisting of a purchase and a sale (or vice versa) of two securities or contracts in the same market, which offset each other. Generally used when referring to commission charges.

Router Hardware that links two computer networks.

RPI Retail Price Index. The UK equivalent of US consumer price inflation (CPI).

RSI Relative Strength Index. RSI is a type of oscillator used by technical analysts to measure the momentum of an instrument or market by comparing the strength of the current price in relation to a previous period.
RSI is a popular indicator because it eliminates the erratic movements seen in other momentum indicators. It is used to identify overbought and oversold signals as well as to act as a warning when divergence exists between the direction of the index and price.
▶ *See also* Momentum *and* Technical Analysis.

Run Up Term for a quick rise in a share price.

RUF Revolving underwriting facility, which allows the borrower to issue short-term notes as required, but containing an in-built underwriting agreement should the market be unable to provide funds.
▶ *See also* NIF.

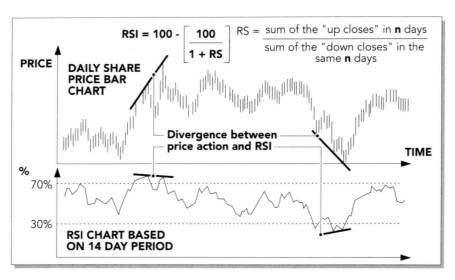

FIGURE 21 RSI

S&P Standard & Poor's. A leading credit rating agency. S&P's assessments of the creditworthiness of borrowers are widely watched in the capital markets.
  ▪ **www.standardandpoors.com** ▪

S&P500 A major barometer of the US stock market. The S&P500 is a market capitalization-weighted arithmetic index representing some 80 per cent of the market value of all issues traded on the New York Stock Exchange.
  It comprises 500 shares, mainly NYSE listed firms. The CME trades futures and futures options on the index. Index options are traded at the CBOE.
  ▪ **www.spglobal.com** ▪
  ▶ *See also* CBOE, CME *and* NYSE.

SA French company title: abbreviation of Société Anonyme. The term is also used in Belgium and Switzerland.

SA Spanish company title: abbreviation of Sociedad Anonima.

SA Italy company title: abbreviation of Societa.

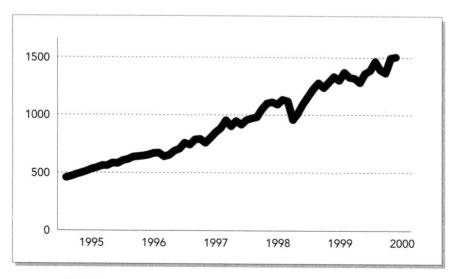

FIGURE 22 S&P 500

SA de CV Mexican company title: abbreviation of Sociedad Anonima de Capital Variable.

SAE Spanish company title: abbreviation of Sociedad Anonima Espanol.

SAFE Synthetic agreement for forward exchange. A collective name for exchange rate agreements (ERA) and forward exchange agreements (FXA).
> *See also* ERA *and* FXA.

Safe Haven Currency A major traded currency, such as the US dollar or Swiss franc, is used by investors and fund managers seeking a safe haven for their funds in times of political turmoil.

SAL Spanish company title: abbreviation of Sociedad Anonima Loboral.

Sallie Mae Student Loan Marketing Association. A publicly traded stock corporation in the US, which guarantees student loans traded on the secondary market. ▪ **www.salliemae.com** ▪

Sample Grade Usually the lowest quality of commodity acceptable for delivery under a futures contract.

Samurai Bond A bond issued in Japan by a foreign borrower denominated in yen. A type of foreign bond.

SARL Portuguese and Brazilian company title: abbreviation of Sociedad Anonima de Responsibiliade Limitada. French company title: abbreviation of Societée à Responsibilitée Limitée. Also used in Luxembourg.

SAS Italian company title: abbreviation of Società in Accomandita Semplice.

S/B Sell after buy limit order. Two orders treated as one, the first order being to buy. If done, the sell order becomes valid.
> *See also* B/S.

SC French company title: abbreviation of Societé en Commandité. Also used in Luxembourg.

Scaleup To sell at regular price intervals in a rising market. Opposite of scaledown.
> *See also* Scaledown.

Scaledown To buy at regular price intervals in a declining market. Opposite of scaleup.
> *See also* Scaleup.

Scalpers ▶ *See* Day Trading.

Scatter Chart In technical analysis, these charts illustrate the degree of correlation between two different instruments in a market showing the value for one plotted against the value of the other. The X axis has values for the first instrument and the Y axis portrays corresponding values for the second instrument. Scatter charts cannot be combined with other analyses on the same graph and limit minders cannot be set for them.
> *See also* Technical Analysis.

SCL Spanish company title: abbreviation of Sociedad Cooperativa Limitada.

Screen Trading Trading conducted via an electronic system.

Scrip Issue A free issue of shares to shareholders when a company transfers money from its reserves to its permanent capital. These new shares are then distributed to the existing holders in proportion to their existing holdings. Also known as a capitalization issue.
> *See also* Capitalization Issue.

SDR Special drawing rights. SDRs are international reserve assets are used by the IMF and countries to supplement existing reserves. They are based on a currency basket of the major traded currencies.
> *See also* IMF *and* ODR.

SEAQ Stock Exchange Automated Quotation. The system used by the London Stock Exchange to trade its shares.

Search Engine A computer program that searches web pages according to a user-defined search string, and displays the results.

Seasonal Adjustment An adjustment that is made to certain economic indicators that tend to have predictable peaks and troughs due to seasonal factors. Seasonal adjustment to an economic indicator makes it easier to discern the underlying.
> *See also* Economic Indicators.

Seasoned Offer Refers to subsequent visits to the capital markets by a company whose stock is already listed. Takes the form of an offer for sale, offer for subscription or a placing.

Seat Term used in derivative markets. Members of an exchange are said to own 'seats' of that exchange. A seat can be bought or sold.

SEC Securities and Exchange Commission, the US regulatory body responsible for oversee alsoing and administering rules associated with all sectors of the securities industry. Its main aim is to promote full public disclosure.
www.sec.gov

SEC filings In the US, companies are required to make SEC on various forms concerning their corporate activities. Some of the forms have also to be filed with the appropriate stock exchange.
> *See also* SEC.

Secondary Market The secondary market provides the liquidity that allows the primary market to function. It is the market where securities are bought and sold once they have been issued.
> *See also* Primary Markets.

Secondary Metals Product of refining scrap or alloys as opposed to primary metals produced from ore.
> *See also* Primary Metals.

Secondary Offering Re-offer of a large block of securities. Often undertaken by the sponsor who initially brought the deal to the market.

Sector Fund A type of mutual fund which invests in one industry or in one geographical area only.

Sector Index A stock exchange composite index that reflects the market activity of a particular industry.

Sectoral Analysts Market analysts who focus on one particular industry. They research specific companies in that sector and make buy and sell recommendations based on that research.

Secular Trend A market movement over the long term which does not reflect seasonal or technical factors.

Securities and Exchange Commission ▶ *See* SEC.

Securities and Futures Association ▶ *See* SFA.

Securitization Pooling various types of loans into standardized securities backed by the loans. The securities can then be traded as a regular security.

Seignorage Revenue raising by governments by printing money. When governments print money they increase the money supply so this can be referred to as an inflation tax.
▶ *See also* Print Money.

Sell-side Used to describe to financial institutions how primary business is trading. The opposite of buy-side.
▶ *See also* Buy-side.

Selloff When severe market pressures depress prices and market instruments are sold to avoid further falls.

Senate Finance Committee Key US Senate committee responsible for tax and other revenue bills.

Senior Secured Debt Secured debt that ranks first for repayment in the event of a default.

Senior Unsecured Debt Securities that have priority ahead of all other unsecured or subordinated debt in ranking for payment in the event of default.

Server A computer at the heart of a network, which can be accessed by any other computers on that network that needs to share its resources.

Settlement Date ▶ *See* Value Date.

Settlement Price ▶ *See* EDSP.

Settlement Risk The risk that an expected settlement amount will not be made on time. The establishment of netting systems is an effort to minimize settlement risk.
▶ *See also* Netting.

SFA The UK Securities and Futures Authority responsible for regulating firms in the securities and futures sectors of the financial services industry. ■ www.sfa.org ■

Share A share represents ownership in a company and the right to receive a share in the profits of that company. Also called a stock.
> *See also* Ordinary Share *and* Preference Share.

Share Discount The amount by which the market value of shares drops below par value. Significant for preferred shares, which pay fixed dividends based on par value.

Share Dividend ▶ *See* Dividend.

Share Premium The amount charged on the market value of shares in excess of par value.

Share Register A central register containing details of a company's share ownership.

Shareholder An individual who holds shares or stock in an organization or company.

Shareholder Value Describes the ability of a company to deliver value to shareholders in terms of both dividends and growth in the company's share price. It focuses on a company's investments and its capacity to generate cash flows from its capital.

Shareholders' Funds Net assets of a company minus the minority interests.
> *See also* Minority Interests.

Shares Per Warrant Ratio A ratio measuring the amount of shares available through the exercise of a warrant.
> *See also* Warrant.

Shareware Freely distributed software. Users do not have to pay for a licence but may be expected to pay a small fee.

Sharpe's Ratio A way to measure risk-adjusted return. It is the ratio of excess portfolio return to portfolio risk where portfolio risk is the standard deviation of the portfolio's returns.
> *See also* Excess Portfolio Returns.

Shelf Registration The US method of registering new issues in advance and having the issue documentation prepared so the stock can be issued quickly.

Shell Company A non-trading company with a stock market quote. Also a dormant unquoted company.

Shogun Bond Public offering in Japan of a non-yen bond by a foreign borrower.

Short Investors are described as being 'short' when they have sold assets in the hope that they can buy them back when prices have fallen. The opposite of long.
> *See also* Long.

Short Bill A bill of exchange payable on demand or within a very short time.

Shortcovering The buying back of a security or asset previously sold so as to close out a short position. Also known as bear covering.

▶ *See also* Short Position.

Short Dated Forwards/Deposits Forward foreign exchange and deposit transactions that show the value date before spot value (O/N, T/N) and from spot (S/N) to one month.

Short First Coupon The first interest payment on a recently issued bond that includes less than the normal semi-annual or annual payment.

Short Hedge The sale of a futures or option position to protect against a fall in price in the corresponding cash market. Opposite of long hedge.

▶ *See also* Hedging.

Short Margin Account An account requiring a margin deposit from investors who are involved in short selling, as opposed to buying on margin.

Short Position A position showing a sale or a greater number of sales over purchases in anticipation of a fall in prices. A short position can be closed out through the purchase of an equivalent amount. Buying back from a short position is known as shortcovering. Selling into a market without a prior long position is called short-selling.

▶ *See also* Long Position.

Short-Selling The selling of instruments that are not held, i.e. with no prior long position, in anticipation of a fall in prices. The action of buying back to cover the short position is known in the market as shortcovering.

▶ *See also* Shortcovering.

SICAV Société d'Investissement à Capital Variable. In France and Luxembourg, these are investment funds similar to mutual funds and unit trusts.

SICOVAM Société Interprofessionnelle pour la Compensation des Valeurs Mobilières is the Paris Stock Exchange clearing organization. SICOVAM settles the securities transaction and the Banque de France settles the cash.

■ www.sicovam.com ■

Sideways Market/Movement Occurs in a market where, for a period of time, price rises and falls are small and restricted to a narrow range. It is also often referred to as a trendless, congested or ranging market.

Sight Draft ▶ *See* Bill of Exchange.

Sight Money ▶ *See* Call Money.

Signalling When a company sends out signals about its future performance. Typical signals would be advance information about expected future earnings and dividend payments.

SIM Italian company title: abbreviation of Società di Intermediazione Mobiliare.

SIMEX The Singapore International Monetary Exchange. It lists interest rate, currency, stock index and crude oil futures. ■ **www.simex.com.sg** ■

Simple Interest The cost of borrowing or the return on lending money, based on the amount borrowed or lent (the principal), length of time the funds are borrowed for, and the market general interest rate level.
    ▶ *See also* Compound Interest.

Simple Moving Average An unweighted moving average.
    ▶ *See also* Moving Average.

Sinking Fund Mandatory prepayments by a borrower regardless of price movements in the secondary bond market to redeem a certain amount of an issue through payments to a special account, thus reducing the principal amount due at maturity.
    ▶ *See also* Pro Rata Sinking Fund *and* Purchase Fund.

S/L A stop loss order. A limit order to buy or sell which operates only when a given price is reached. Such an order is normally placed to cut losses on an existing position. Once the stop loss level is reached, the order is often executed at the next market price (particularly in volatile markets).

SL Spanish company title: abbreviation of Società Limitada.

SMI Swiss Market Index. The SMI consists of 24 securities (bearer shares and participation certificates) from 20 major Swiss companies quoted on the Basel, Geneva and Zurich Stock Exchanges. It is a 'chain' index weighted by the market capitalization of its constituent securities. The SMI is the basis of the index options traded on Eurex.

S/N Abbreviation for spot/next. Used in swap and deposit transactions when the first value date is spot value and maturity falls on the next working day.
    ▶ *See also* Swap.

SNC Italian company title meaning Società in Nome, Collectivo.

SOFFEX Formerly the Swiss Options and Financial Futures Exchange, which merged with the German exchange DTB to create Eurex.
    ▶ *See also* EUREX.

Society for Worldwide Interbank Financial Telecommunication ▶ *See* SWIFT.

Soft Loan Carries an interest rate below the real cost of borrowing, or no interest rate at all. The IDA – the World Bank affiliate – provides soft loans to developing countries for long-term capital projects.
    ▶ *See also* IDA.

Softs Soft commodities such as sugar, coffee and cocoa.

Sogo Sosha Very large Japanese trading companies.

Solvency When a company can meet all its debts when they fall due. Opposite of insolvency.
    ▶ *See also* Insolvency.

Sour Crude High-sulphur-content crude oil.

Sour Gas Natural or associated gas, which has a high sulphur content.

Sovereign Issue A bond issued by a government-backed agency.

SpA Italian company title: abbreviation of Società per Azioni

Special Drawing Rights *See* SDR.

Specialist Market makers in one or more selected securities listed on an exchange. Found at a trading post on the floor they earn their income from commission when acting as a broker or from the spread in their quoted prices when acting as a dealer.

Specifications Refers to properties of a given crude oil or refined petroleum product. Properties are specified because they often vary widely, even within the same grade of product.

Speculation Taking relatively high risks in financial markets in the hope of making large gains. Speculation involves trying to anticipate the future when making investments.

Speculator An investor who practices speculation. A speculator tries to anticipate price changes with a view to making profits. Generally, the speculator has no long-term interest in the securities or assets they trade in.
  See also Hedging.

Speedline In technical analysis, speedlines measure the rate of rise or fall in a trend and are constructed by dividing trends into thirds and drawing trendlines at key levels.
  See also Technical Analysis.

Spin Off Method used by a company to split its operations and assets by proportionately distributing shares it holds in another to its own shareholders. Also termed hive off.

Sponsor Term used for the investment or merchant bank that advises on, makes prices and brings a new issue to the market.

Spontaneous Lending New lending that is not intended to provide the funds needed to repay interest and principal on pre-existing loans.

Spot Market A market whose trades deliver and settle immediately (normally two working days after the trade). Also known as cash market and physical market.

Spot Month The nearest dated futures contract.
  See also Contract Month *and* Futures.

Spot Next *See* S/N.

Spread Difference in a price quotation between the bid and the ask. A large spread usually means the market lacks liquidity.

Spread can also be used to express the difference in yields between two fixed income securities of the same quality but different maturities, or of different quality but the same maturities.

A futures spread is the difference in prices between delivery months in the same or different markets.

Spread Trading The purchase of one futures contract and the simultaneous sale of another in order to take advantage of expected price discrepancies.

Square Position ▶ *See* Flat.

Squeeze A squeeze occurs when prices are being forced up or down as investors rush to cut their losses. Also used to describe a period when monetary policy is tight.

SRL Italian company title: abbreviation of Società Responsibilità Limitata.

Stag Operator who applies for a new security hoping to sell it, on allotment at a premium over the issue price.

Stagflation An economy where high inflation is accompanied by high unemployment and stagnant economic activity.

Standard & Poor's ▶ *See* S&P.

Standard Deviation A statistical measure of the degree to which an individual value in a spread of values may vary from the mean or average of that spread. Used as a method of assessing risk factors.

Standby Credit Arrangement with a lender (a group of banks or the IMF in the case of a member country) whereby a fixed amount of credit will be available for drawing during a given period, if required.

Standby Loan The basic IMF sovereign loan, usually over one or two years, aimed at overcoming short-term balance of payments difficulties. Loan conditions are focused on macro-economic policies.

State Planning Government regulation of a sector of the economy using state appointed administrators who do not bow to free market forces.

▶ *See also* Market Economy, Mixed Economy *and* Planned Economy.

Statement of Cash Flows A financial account that shows the cash flows generated by a company's operations, investments and financing activities. Sometimes called the flow of funds statement or the source and applications of funds statement.

Ste Cve Belgian company title: abbreviation of Società Cooperataive.

Stochastics Used in technical analysis, stochastics is a momentum indicator which identifies possible changes in trends in sideways moving markets. There are two types – fast and slow.

▶ *See also* Technical Analysis.

Stock A stock represents ownership in a company and the right to receive a share in the profits of that company. Also called a share.
> *See also* Ordinary Share *and* Preference Share.

Stock Average An arithmetic average. Also referred to as an index.
> *See also* Stock Index.

Stock Broker A company, or individual, executing trades, and/or investment advice, to the customer base, both individual and institutional while not acting as a principal.

Stock Dividend A dividend paid to shareholders in the form of authorized but hitherto unissued shares.
> *See also* Dividend.

Stock Exchange A trading-floor or screen-based auction market where exchange members gather to buy and sell securities.

Stock Exchange Automated Quotation ▶ *See* SEAQ.

Stock Index A market index is a numerical representation of the way an entire market has performed relative to some 'base' reference date in the past. Composite measure of the movement stock indices are calculated in two ways – weighted or unweighted. Unweighted indices are simple arithmetic or geometric averages. In Weighted indices, certain stocks carry a greater weighting than others, usually based on their market value or capitalization.
> *See also* Capitalisation-Weighted Index.

Stock Index Fund A fund that invests in a group of securities from a particular stock market index.

Stock Lending Lending of shares by long-term holders such as institutions when shares are in short supply. Often an investment house will not actually take delivery of the stock but will use it as an underlying instrument in a derivatives strategy.

Stock Option ▶ *See* Equity Options.

Stock Split The break up of a share into smaller units, which does not affect either share capital or reserves. Opposite of a reverse stock split.
> *See also* Reverse Stock Split.

Stop Loss/Stop Limit Order ▶ *See* S/L.

Straddle An option strategy involving one call and one put with the same strike and same expiry date.

Straight Bond ▶ *See* Bullet Bond.

Strangle An option strategy involving one call and one put with different strike levels but with the same expiry date.

Street Name ▶ *See* Nominee Account.

Strike Price The price agreed in an options transaction and at which the option may be exercised. Also known as the exercise price.

Structural Adjustment Reform of the structure of a whole economy. Mostly used in the context of structural adjustment programmes promoted by the IMF and the World Bank. Designed to bring about open markets, liberalized trade and to lower budget and current account deficits.

Student Loan Marketing Association *See* Sallie Mae.

Subordinated Debt Debt that ranks for repayment of principal behind debt senior to it.

Subsidiary A company of which more than 50 per cent of its voting stock is owned by the parent company.

Sunshine Laws Laws in the USA that allow maximum public disclosures on governmental bodies and include organizations in charge of securities trading regulations.

Super Voting Share A type of share capital structure not often seen outside the USA in which certain shares, on being issued, give the holder increased voting rights.

Supply/Demand The amount of sellers providing supplies to a market and buyers creating demand. Supply and demand is a major influence in generating the market price.

Supply-side Economics Theory that tax cuts, and similar measures, will boost investment in production and increase the supply of goods in the economy.

Support Support is a level, usually identified on a price chart, where buying interest is strong enough to overcome selling pressure so that the price does not fall beyond the support level. Each time a level of support is penetrated it can take on a new level of support.

▶ *See also* Resistance *and* Trendline.

Supranational Agency which raises money in world capital markets to fund investment in developing countries or large projects. Supranationals are 'owned' by a consortium of national governments. They include the World Bank and EBRD.

Surplus The difference when income or revenue is greater than expenditure. Opposite of deficit.

▶ *See also* Deficit.

Sushi Bond Non-yen bond issued abroad by a Japanese company to Japanese residents. These bonds offer a way for Japanese companies to increase foreign currency holdings.

Suspension A company's shares can be temporarily suspended, either voluntarily by the company or by the relevant stock exchange, when a key announcement is expected. Longer or permanent suspension can be imposed by a stock exchange for failure to comply with listing requirements or numerous other reasons.

SVTs Spécialistes en Valeurs du Trésor, established in 1987. Comprises a group of banks and brokers who are primary dealers and market makers in French government bond markets.

Swap An exchange of cash flows between two counterparties designed to offset interest rate or currency risk. A swap is arranged as a single transaction but consists of two legs when the exchange of cash flows occur.

Swaption An option on a swap, giving the holder the right, but not the obligation, to enter into an interest rate swap as either the payer or receiver of the fixed side of the swap.
▶ *See also* Swap.

Sweet Crude Crude oil with a low sulphur content such as those from North Africa, Nigeria and the North Sea.

SWIFT The Society for Worldwide Interbank Financial Telecommunication. Operates a standard network for effecting international banking transactions. ■ **www.swift.com** ■

SWIFT Codes The coded instructions used by SWIFT for effecting international banking transactions over its network.
▶ *See also* SWIFT.

Swing Line A credit facility allowing borrowers to take money overnight.

Swiss Market Index ▶ *See* SMI.

Switch The exchanging of one security for another. A switch is often used to improve a portfolio, perhaps to enhance the yield or quality.

Syndicate Group of institutions responsible for issuing debt. A syndicate assembles to share the risk of an issue and split it into manageable amounts.

Syndicated Loan A large loan arranged by a group of banks that form a syndicate, headed by the lead manager.

Systematic Risk Risk that cannot be diversified away as it is the risk of market movements or of market segment movements. Also known as market risk.

Systemic Risk The risk associated with an adverse change in the overall financial system.

T

T/N Abbreviation for tomorrow/next or tom/next. Used in swap and deposit transactions when the first value date is tomorrow (tom) and maturity falls on the next working day (spot). The T/N swap price is adjusted for the interest rate differential in that short period.

Takedown To receive and accept an allotment of securities in the primary market.

Takeover Acquisition of a controlling interest in a company through the purchase of its shares.

Takeover Bid The initial offer by a predator company for another. The bid can be in cash, shares or a combination. Bids usually have a closing date for acceptance.

Taking a Position The act of buying or selling to establish a long or short position.

Tan Book A six-weekly survey of the outlook for the US economy published by the Fed. Also known as the beige book.

Tangibles ▶ See Assets/Liabilities.

Tankan The Bank of Japan's quarterly corporate survey with a wide range of other corporate data. It includes the closely watched diffusion index for major manufacturers, which compares the ratio of those who expect business to improve to those who expect it to worsen. The lower the index, the gloomier the outlook. The tankan is an important reference for the central bank in formulating monetary policy.

Tankoku Japanese government paper with maturities of three and six months. Introduced in 1986 to help smooth out refunding of huge amounts of previously issued ten-year government bonds.

Taxation Risk The risk that tax laws relating to dividend income and capital gains on shares might change, making stocks less attractive.

TCP/IP Acronym for transmission control protocol/internet protocol. Key protocols that govern the transmission of data and information across networks.

Technical Analysis A method of predicting the future direction of prices by studying charts of past market action. Technical analysts or chartists pay close attention to recurring patterns in the price action, to price trends and their speed or momentum. The technical analyst predicts future prices on the basis of how prices move up and down, rather than why. Looking at the historical evolution of market prices, trading volumes and other indicators of trading activity, the technical analyst predicts future prices from price action itself rather than by looking at fundamental data. The analysts use four basic types of charts – line, bar, candlestick, and point and figure. And there are a large number of technical theories and indicators including Elliott Wave, RSI, moving average and stochastics.

▶ *See also* Bar Chart, Candlestick Chart, Dow Theory, Elliott Wave Theory, Fundamental Analysis, Line Chart, Moving Average, Resistance *and* Support.

TED spread Abbreviation for Treasury Eurodollar Spread. This is the yield difference between US Treasury bill and Eurodollar futures contracts and is a widely followed spread trade.

▶ *See also* Spread Trading.

Tender The process in a securities market, whereby all allocations are assigned at the same price. In commodities trading, it is the notice of intent to deliver physical goods against a futures contract.

Tender Offer A company making a tender offer requires applicants to state the number of securities they require plus the price they are prepared to pay for them. Once all applications have been received, the company fixes a single 'striking price' at which the securities will be allotted to applicants at that price or higher. Also known as an offer for subscription.

Tender Price Price offered by investors at which they are willing to buy a new issue. The issuing house usually sets predetermined limits within which the tender price can be made.

Tenderable Grades Grades designated as deliverable to settle a futures contract. Also called deliverable grades.

Term CD Certificate of deposit that carry maturities from two to five years.

▶ *See also* CD.

Term Repo A repo lasting for 30 days or longer and used to hedge a position for a similar amount of time.

▶ *See also* Repo.

Term Sheet Document that legally defining the details of a loan or rescheduling agreement and signed by all participants.

Terminal Onshore installation designed to receive oil/gas from a pipeline or from tankers. It is not a refinery.

Terminal Market Commodity market where physicals are exchanged for cash and are deliverable against maturing futures contracts.

Terminal Value The assumed value of a business at the end of a forecasting period, usually after ten years of projected earnings.

Theta A measure of change in the value of an option compared with the continuous decrease in time to expiry. Also known as time decay.

▶ *See also* Option.

Thin Market A market where there is little buying or selling interest, with low volume or activity. Can apply to a whole market or a single instrument.

Three Box Reversal In technical analysis, a much used point and figure chart for intermediate analysis which needs only the high and low prices for the day.
> *See also* Point and Figure Charts *and* Technical Analysis.

Throughput Total volume of raw materials processed in a given period by a plant such as an oil refinery. Also, the total volume of crude oil and refined products handled by a storage facility or pipeline.

Tick The minimum movement possible in the price of a financial instrument.
> *See also* Basis Point.

Ticker Symbol Letters that identify a stock traded on a stock exchange.
> *See also* Ticker Tape.

Ticker Tape An electronic display showing prices at which each successive trade is executed on a stock exchange, the trading volume and the share symbols.
> *See also* Ticker Symbol.

Tier One Under capital adequacy standards set for commercial banks by the Bank for International Settlements, at least half of the 8 per cent of capital required to be set against risk-weighted assets must be core capital. This comprises equity and disclosed reserves. So-called supplementary capital, or tier two, constitutes the rest. This includes undisclosed reserves, general provisions against loan losses, subordinated term debt and hybrid capital instruments combining characteristics of debt and equity. Also known as core capital.
> *See also* BIS *and* Capital Adequacy.

Tier Two ▷ *See* Tier One.

TIFFE The Tokyo International Financial Futures Exchange. The exchange trades interest rate and currency futures. ▪ **www.tiffe.or.jp** ▪

Tigers Collective term used in the 1990s to describe fast-developing economies of South-East Asia including Indonesia, Malaysia, Taiwan and Thailand.

Time Decay ▷ *See* Theta.

Time Deposit ▷ *See* CD.

Time Draft ▷ *See* Bill of Exchange.

Time Series A series of values over consecutive periods of time. Used in financial markets to describe price histories.

Time Value The component of an option premium which takes into consideration the time to expiry and the volatility of the underlying.
> *See also* Intrinsic Value.

TOCOM The Tokyo Commodities Exchange, Japan's largest commodity exchange. ▇ www.tocom.or.jp ▇

Tokyo International Financial Futures Exchange ▶ *See* TIFFE.

Tokyo Stock Exchange ▶ *See* TSE.

TomNext ▶ *See* T/N.

Tombstone A public notice such as a newspaper advertisement announcing the details of a new issue including the names of investment and finance houses who have organized and provided the funds. A tombstone appears as a matter of record and is not as an invitation to subscribe.

Top Down An investment strategy that tries to achieve a balance in the weightings of various sectors or industries. If a fund uses a top-down approach it will look at general economic or market trends to find the best sectors to invest in. Then it will look for the best investments within that sector. Opposite of bottom up.
▶ *See also* Bottom Up.

Top Line Net sales/total revenues or adjective for action aimed to affect net sales/revenues.
▶ *See also* Bottom Line.

Top Reversal A top reversal day would be the setting of a new high in an uptrend followed by a lower close than the previous day's closing rate (sometimes the previous two days).

Total Return Total return is the dividend plus any capital gains or losses achieved by investing in a stock, expressed in annualized terms as a percentage of the amount invested.

Touch The best (highest) bid and (lowest) offer in a security currently available in the market. This need not be the two-way price of one market maker but is taken by looking at the market prices submitted by all market makers.

Tracking Share A tracking share or stock is created by a company for a subsidiary. It trades separately from the parent company's stock but does not carry any voting rights. It enables the company to compensate staff or raise funds to make acquisitions. It is popular among established companies who risk losing staff to new start-ups because it can offer a stake in the business to employees.

Trade Barrier Artificial restraint on the free exchange of goods and services between countries, usually in the form of tariffs, subsidies, quotas or exchange controls.

Trade Balance ▶ *See* Balance of Trade.

Trade Bill ▶ *See* Bill of Exchange.

This announcement appears as a matter of record only.

February 10, 2000

BMW Group

BMW US Capital Corp.
Wilmington, Delaware, United States of America

USD 250,000,000
7.375% Notes due 2003
Issue Price: 101.177%

USD 400,000,000
Floating Rate Notes due 2003
Issue Price: 100.010%

unconditionally and irrevocably guaranteed by

Bayerische Motoren Werke Aktiengesellschaft
Munich, Federal Republic of Germany

ABN AMRO	**HypoVereinsbank**

Bank of America International Limited	**Bayerische Landesbank Girozentrale**	**BNP Paribas Group**
Credit Suisse First Boston	**DG BANK** Deutsche Genossenschaftsbank AG	**Dresdner Kleinwort Benson**
Merrill Lynch International	**Nomura International**	**Warburg Dillon Read**

FIGURE 23 Tombstone

Trade Weighted Used in reference to foreign exchange rates, with currency movements weighted in accordance with their importance in a country's trade. This trade weighting is then formulated in an index.

Trading House Concern that buys and sells futures and physicals for the account of customers as well as for its own account.

Trading Floor ▶ *See* Floor.

Trading Post In the US, the structure (the post) on the floor of a stock exchange at which market makers buy and sell securities.

Trading Range The high and low trading points of an instrument over a period of time. Often referred to as the hi/lo. Chartists watch to see if the price of a financial instrument breaks through its trading high or low since this can be a portent for its future trend.

Trading Volume A generic term used to describe the total number of securities or contracts traded in any particular period.

Tranche French word for a slice. Used widely to mean a portion, allocation or instalment.

Transaction Fees Charges payable by investors on purchases and sales of securities.

Translation Risk A form of currency risk associated with the valuation of balance sheet assets and liabilities between financial reporting dates.

Treasury Bill Short-term government security issued in domestic currency with maturities not exceeding one year and therefore considered to be a money market instrument. Treasury bills are sold at a discount from par and do not carry a coupon.

Treasury Bond Government debt security issued with a maturity of ten years or more traded in the capital markets. Treasury bonds are issued with a fixed coupon.

Treasury Note Government debt security issued with maturities of two to ten years and traded in the capital markets. Treasury notes bear a fixed coupon.

Trend Reversal ▶ *See* Reversal Day.

Trendline In technical analysis, a trendline is a line connecting specific price action to identify the direction of the market. The longer the trendline has been in place, tested but not broken, the more significant it becomes.
 ▶ *See also* Technical Analysis.

Triangles In technical analysis triangles are price patterns usually interpreted as a continuation signal. They represent a pause in the existing trend, after which the original trend resumes. Triangles usually take longer than a month to form but generally less than three months.
 ▶ *See also* Technical Analysis.

Trigger Option A type of barrier option.
> ▶ *See also* Down and In *and* Up and In.

Trigger Price The price at which buy/sell mechanisms in commodity agreements take effect.

Triple A Rated ▶ *See* AAA/Aaa.

Triple Top/Bottom In technical analysis, a price pattern similar to the head and shoulders except that the three peaks or troughs are at about the same level.
> ▶ *See also* Head and Shoulders *and* Technical Analysis.

Triple Witching Occurs every quarter and is the simultaneous expiry of stock index futures contracts, stock index options and options on individual stocks. It can often increase volatility, notably on the US stock markets.

Trustee Institution appointed to ensure all terms and conditions of the bond indenture are fully adhered to.

TSE The Tokyo Stock Exchange. ■ **www.tse.or.jp** ■

Turnover Also known as sales or revenue turnover is the amount of income derived from a company's provision of mainstream goods and services.

Two-way Market Market where dealers actively quote both buying and selling rates.

UCITS Undertakings for collective investments in transferable securities. A European Community regulation governing any collective fund, such as a unit trust, sold within the Community.

UNCTAD United Nations Conference on Trade and Development. An organization that promotes better international trading conditions for developing countries to raise their standard of living. It used to be a forum for most commodity price stabilization pacts.
- **www.unctad.org**

Undercapitalized Term used when a business is not supplied with enough funds by its owners to support its activities and provide for any needed expansion.

Underlying Used in derivative markets to describe the financial instrument or physical commodity on which a futures or options contract is based.
- *See also* Derivatives.

Undersubscribed Whereby a new issue is not completely bought by investors. Opposite of oversubscribed.
- *See also* Oversubscribed.

Undervalued When a security or currency is trading at a price lower than it should, relative to fundamental factors. Opposite to overvalued.
- *See also* Overvalued.

Underwriter ▶ *See* Lead Manager/Underwriter.

Underwriting A form of insurance whereby, an underwriter agrees for a fee to take up a specific quantity of a new issue at the issue price if there is insufficient demand.

Unemployment When people capable of working are unable to find work. There are two main types of unemployment. Frictional unemployment is the temporary unemployment caused by the time it takes people to find new jobs. Structural unemployment refers to the mismatch between vacancies and labour supply caused by structural economic change.

Uniform resource locator ▶ *See* URL.

Unit trust ▶ *See* Mutual Fund.

United Nations Conference on Trade and Development ▶ *See* UNCTAD.

Unlimited Liability Where no restriction applies to an owner's losses in a business.

Unlisted Stock A security that is not listed or traded on a stock exchange floor.

Unmatched Book One in which the maturities of assets and liabilities do not correspond, specifically when the average maturity of the liabilities is less than that of the assets.

Unrealized Gain/Profit Loss The profit or loss that would be reported, should a position be liquidated.

Unweighted/Weighted Indices Stock indices are calculated in two ways – they are either weighted or unweighted. Unweighted indices are simple arithmetic or geometric averages. Weighted indices are those in which certain stocks carry a greater weighting than others. This weighting is usually based on the market value or capitalization of those stocks.

Unwinding a Position A position (long or short) is unwound, or reversed, by an offsetting transaction to result in a square or flat position.

Up and In A trigger option that is activated when the price of the underlying rises to a pre-determined level.
> *See also* Option.

Up and Out A knockout option that is cancelled when the price of the underlying rises above a pre-determined level.
> *See also* Option.

Upgrade Upward regrade of credit status for a borrowing institution or its debt instruments. Opposite of downgrade.
> *See also* Downgrade.

Upstream Prospecting, drilling for, and production from, the wellhead to the pipeline or to the tanker loading terminal of crude oil or natural gas.

Uptrend/Downtrend In technical analysis both an uptrend and a downtrend are defined as trends that can be drawn on chart by joining a minimum of four points.
> *See also* Technical Analysis.

Uruguay Round World trade negotiations that created the World Trade Organization.
> *See also* WTO.

URL Uniform resource locator. The address of a web page.

US Street Method The standard yield to maturity calculation used by the US market participants except the US Treasury, whereby the yield is compounded semi-annually despite the coupon frequency.

US Treasury Bill Short-term US government bearer securities with maturities of three, six and maximum 12 months. Sold on a regular basis and commanding a dominating position on money markets. Nearly one-third of marketable US Treasury debt is concentrated in Treasury bills. The purchase and sale of such bills through open market operations forms a key part of US monetary policy.

US Treasury Bond Long-term US Treasury securities with maturities of ten years or more. Treasury bonds make up 15 per cent of marketable debt. Like Treasury notes, they pay a semi-annual coupon, so they are also known as coupon securities.

US Treasury Note US Treasury securities with maturities from two to ten years. Notes are non-callable and make up more than 50 per cent of marketable debt. They pay a fixed semi-annual coupon and mature at par.

USDA US Department of Agriculture which implements agricultural policy and is a major source of forecasts and statistics on agriculture in the US and world-wide. ▪ **www.usda.gov** ▪

Utilities State or private-sector enterprises providing public services such as gas, electricity and water.

Value Date The date on which either the security or cash equivalent is settled on completion of a trade.

Variable Rate A periodically adjusted rate, usually based on a standard market rate.

Variable Redemption Bond A bond whose redemption value is linked to a variable such as the dollar/yen exchange rate, the performance of the US Treasury 30-year bond, a stock index or the gold price. Often issued in bull and bear portions, or tranches.

Variation Margin Variation margin is collected on a daily basis by clearing houses or brokers to ensure margin requirements on a particular transaction keep pace with subsequent market movements. It represents a running profit or loss on a contract. It is calculated by revaluing all positions with reference to the closing prices each day.
> *See also* Margin *and* Mark to Market.

Vega The measure of change in the value of the option compared with a change in volatility.
> *See also* Option.

Venture Capital Funds used to invest in small companies that are considered to be in their first phase of growth. Funding is provided by private and institutional investors.

Vertical Spread An option strategy.
> *See also* Option.

Virus Computer code or a program designed to have negative effects on the computer or computer network it infects.

Volatility Volatility describes the degree to which a value such as a stock price or an interest rate changes over a specified time period. High volatility means that the value changes dramatically, usually due to high market uncertainty. Traders thrive on market volatility because it presents many opportunities to earn a profit.
Low volatility means values change minimally, as is the case when all news has been priced into the market. Professional investors tend to benefit from low volatility because they are better able to lock in stable returns.

The financial markets distinguish between historical volatility and implied volatility. Historical volatility is a measure of volatility based on past price or yield behaviour, while implied volatility is implied by the price of an option.

Volatility Analysis   Volatility analysis measures the rate of random change in market prices.

Volatility Index   Used in technical analysis. A trend-following analysis that measures the average price movement per interval.

▶ *See* Technical Analysis.

Volume-Weighted Average Price ▶ *See* VWAP.

Voting Trust   A trust set up by the company at a commercial bank inviting ordinary shareholders to deposit their shares for a fixed period in return for other privileges. This procedure is carried out if a company has financial instability and board members wish to concentrate voting power to make rapid policy changes.

VTC   A voting trust certificate. Issued by a voting trust, a negotiable certificate proving that ordinary shares have been deposited into the trust and so ordinary shareholders have relinquished their right to vote.

VWAP   Volume-weighted average price. VWAP is a method of pricing transactions and a benchmark to measure the efficiency of institutional trading or the performance of traders. VWAP represents the total value of stocks traded in a particular security on a given day, divided by the total volume of stocks traded in that security on that day. Calculation techniques vary: some will use data from all markets or just the primary market and may or may not adjust for resubmits and other error corrections. It is also known as dynamic time and sales.

WACC ▶ Weighted Average Cost of Capital. WACC is used to measure whether a potential investment will generate an adequate return. It is the weighted cost of debt and equity.

Wall Street Colloquial name for the New York Stock Exchange that has loosely come to mean securities trading generally in the US.

Wall Street Refiner A Wall Street investment firm that buys or sells crude oil and petroleum products – as futures contracts or paper barrels – on a scale similar to real refineries. Typically these investment firms do not own oil refineries and take no actual delivery of oil.

Warehousing Process whereby a group of investors independently buys shares in a company but each investor keeps his holding below the official notification threshold. This can be a surreptitious method of mounting a takeover bid.
▶ *See also* Acting in Concert.

Warrant A type of financial instrument attached to a security that has a separate life and value. A warrant allows the investor to purchase ordinary shares at a fixed price over a period of time (years) or to perpetuity. The price of the shares is usually higher than the market price at the time of issue. A warrant is freely transferable and can be traded separately.

Webmaster The person in charge of the administration of a web site.

Wedges Used in technical analysis. This pattern is similar to a symmetrical triangle. Wedges are usually seen within the existing trend and are generally continuation patterns. The wedge usually lasts more than a month but not more than three months.

Weighted Average Cost of Capital ▶ *See* WACC.

Weighted Average Coupon The weighted average coupon rate of all the loan rates of the underlying collateral in a pool of mortgages.

Weighted Average Maturity The weighted average maturity of all the loans making up the underlying collateral in a mortgage pool.

Weighted Index ▶ *See* Unweighted/Weighted Indices.

Weighting The weight, or importance, given to the various constituent components of an index or economic indicator.

Wet Barrels Term used in oil trading that means delivery of a product rather than the transfer of a tanker receipt. Describes oil that has shipping dates ascribed to it.

When Issued ▶ *See* W/I.

Whisper Estimates Informal earnings forecasts for high profile blue chip companies. Whisper numbers are generally above the consensus estimates collated and published by earnings tracking companies. A company will often see its stock sold off if it fails to meet whisper numbers even though it matches the published consensus figures.
> ▶ *See also* Consensus Estimates.

White Knight A potential friendly acquirer sought out by a company to protect it from a hostile takeover.
> ▶ *See also* Poison Pill *and* Pac Man Defence.

W/I When Issued. When, as and if issued. W/I trading starts immediately after the formal announcement of issues. Instruments are delivered when issued. They are traded on what is known as the grey market. No interest accrues during this period. Also known as free to trade.

Wide Opening When the spread between buying and selling prices is unusually wide.

Williams Percent R Used in technical analysis. This oscillator is like a stochastic since it measures the latest close in relation to its price range over a set number of days. Named after its originator, Larry Williams.
> ▶ *See also* Technical Analysis.

Windfall Profit An unusual profit, normally as the result of a specific, one-off situation.

Window Shortened reference to a Federal Reserve Bank discount window.
> ▶ *See also* Federal Reserve System.

Window Dressing Dates Window dressing dates are ends of periods, usually a year end but can be three or six months, when banks and companies aim to present their accounts in a favourable light, often helped by raising additional short-term funds.

Withholding Tax Tax deducted at source on interest or dividend payments to be paid by the investor.

Working Capital Usually refers to net working capital and is the resource that a company can use to finance day-to-day operations. It is calculated by taking current liabilities from current assets.
> ▶ *See also* Assets/Liabilities.

Working Control Theoretically more than 50 per cent of all voting shares is needed to control a company. However, if the holder has a substantial minority interest then it could have effective (working) control if the rest of the company's stock was all held in small shareholdings.

World Bank The World Bank is an agency for channelling aid funds, usually medium term, for capital and human resource projects to developing nations. The World Bank can raise private funds and make loans from its own resources. It also raises money by selling bonds on the world capital markets.

▶ *See also* Bretton Woods.

World Trade Organization ▶ *See* WTO.

World Wide Web ▶ *See* WWW.

Write Off Book-keeping action that at one stroke depreciates an asset out of the balance sheet.

WTI West Texas Intermediate is a benchmark crude against which other crudes are priced. A light (40 degrees API) sweet blend of crude oils produced in fields in Western Texas. The benchmark for US crude oil.

WTO World Trade Organization. ▪ **www.wto.orgiza** ▪

▶ *See also* GATT *and* Uruguay Round.

WWW World Wide Web. A global system of servers that supplies the infrastructure for the Internet.

XML Extensible mark-up language. XML is a new standard for the transfer of information over the Internet and is expected to replace HTML.

▶ *See also* HTML.

Yankee Bond Dollar bond issued in the US, by a foreign borrower, registered with the SEC. A type of foreign bond.
  ▶ *See also* SEC.

Yard Currency market term used when dealing one thousand million units of a currency. In foreign exchange, used to refer to yen and lira. Based on the French word milliard.

Year Bill ▶ *See* US Treasury Bill.

Year on Year Rate A rate that compares the current reporting period (e.g. a month or quarter) with the same period a year earlier.

Yield Percentage return on an investment, usually at an annual rate.

Yield Curve (including Positive and Negative) The graphical representation of the yields of a set of bonds or other instruments with the same credit risk and currency but different maturities.
  There are many different yield curves, including government benchmark curves, deposit curves, swap curves, and credit curves. Benchmark curves consist of securities that meet certain criteria for liquidity, size, price availability and other characteristics, such as turnover rate. These securities set standards for the market against which other issues can be measured.
  A yield curve is not static and can change quickly at any time. For example, a word or two from a central banker can fuel expectations of higher inflation, which may cause longer-term debt prices to fall more than short-term prices. If the yield curve is positive sloping it will steepen as the longer yields move up more than the shorter ones.
  There are four fundamental yield curve shapes: – normal, flat, inverted and humped.
  ▶ *See also* Maturity

Yield Gap Also known as yield ratio. This ratio is calculated by subtracting the dividend yield on equities from the yield on long-term government bonds.
  ▶ *See also* Yield.

Yield to Maturity ▶ *See* YTM.

YTM Yield To Maturity. A key consideration when comparing bond investments. It is the annualized rate of return of a bond, namely the interest rate that makes the present value of the a bond's future cash equal to the present price of the bond. It assumes the bond will be held to maturity and that the coupons will be reinvested at the same rate.

Yours Dealers' language. The dealer hits the bid quoted by his counterparty. It has to be qualified by the amount. Confirms the act of selling.

Zero Cost Option An option strategy whereby the cost of purchasing an option is totally offset by the premium generated from the sale of an option. Both premiums are therefore identical.

▶ *See also* Risk Reversal.

Zero Coupon Bond A bond that pays no coupon but is issued at a deep discount to face value. The difference between the issue and redemption prices creates a hefty capital gain, which boosts the yield close to market levels. As it does not pay a coupon, investors do not run the risk of reinvesting interest paid at a lower rate if interest rates fall during the life of the bond.

Zero Coupon Swap An interest rate swap in which one party makes regular payments while the other party makes one lump sum payment, typically at the end of the contract.

Zero Coupon Yield Curve A yield curve of zero coupon bonds. Market practice is often to derive this curve theoretically from the par yield curve. Frequently used to derive discount factors. Also known as spot yield curve.

▶ *See also* Yield Curve.